THE SUPPORTERS GUIDE TO FOOTBALL LEAGUE (
(8th Edition)

FOREWORD

As we approach our tenth year of publication, the FA's Super League proposal is causing concern amongst clubs in the Second, Third and Fourth Divisions and, looking back over our previous editions, I find that, every year, Football always seems to be facing some such uncertainty! There is no doubt that these problems will be solved and, considering that over the last five seasons average attendances have increased as follows:- Division 2 from 9,021 to 11,374; Division 3 from 3,210 to 5,138 and Division 4 from 3,107 to 3,218, I believe that the future is bright.

In 1992 we will be publishing a new book THE SUPPORTERS' GUIDE TO NON-LEAGUE FOOTBALL CLUBS as we have had many requests for additional information about the country's semi-professional sides.

We are, as usual, indebted to the staffs of the 219 clubs included in this guide for their co-operation. Special thanks also go to Chris Ambler for the photographs and to Roy Adlard.

Finally, a brief word about this edition of the guide. When we began this publication in 1982, I did not realise quite how details would change each year and this year is no exception with over 40 changes in the road directions alone! Disabled supporters are now much better catered for with the majority of Football League Clubs providing separate facilities including special toilets. I look forward to the day when every club will have a purpose-built section catering for disabled fans.

We wish our readers a happy and safe spectating season.

FURTHER COPIES OF THE GUIDE CAN BE OBTAINED DIRECTLY FROM THE ADDRESS SHOWN BELOW.

John Robinson — Editor

INDEX

BRITISH LIBRARY
CATALOGUING IN
PUBLICATION DATA

The Supporters' Guide to Football League Clubs — 8th Edition
1. Great Britain. Football League Football Clubs — Robinson, editor
I. Robinson, John 1947.
796. 334'63'02541
ISBN 0-947808-16-7

Printed by Adlard Print & Typesetting Services, The Old School, The Green, Ruddington, Notts. NG11 6HH

WEMBLEY STADIUM

Opened: 1923
Location: Wembley, Middx. HA9 ODW
Telephone: Box Office (081) 900 1234
Telephone: Administration (081) 902 8833

Ground Capacity: 80,000
Seating Capacity: 80,000
Record Attendance: 100,000
Pitch Size: 115 x 75 yds

GENERAL INFORMATION
Guided Tours Available: Telephone (081) 902 8833
Parking: Car Park for over 7,000 vehicles
Nearest Railway Stations: Wembley Park, Wembley Central, Wembley Complex (5-10 minutes walk)
Nearest Police Station: Mobile Unit in front of Twin Towers
Police Force Responsible For Crowd Control: Metropolitan

GROUND INFORMATION
All Sections of the Ground are Covered
Family Facilities: Location of Stand:
Family Enclosure, North Stand

DISABLED SUPPORTERS INFORMATION
Wheelchairs: Limited Facilities available to ticket holders
Disabled Toilets: Yes
The Blind: No Special Facilities

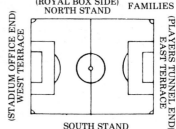

OLYMPIC WAY & TWIN TOWERS
(ROYAL BOX SIDE)
NORTH STAND   FAMILIES

(STADIUM OFFICE END)
WEST TERRACE

(PLAYERS TUNNEL END)
EAST TERRACE

SOUTH STAND

How to get to Wembley By Road

2

ALDERSHOT FC

Founded: 1926	**Record Attendance:** 19,138 (28/1/70)
Turned Professional: 1927	**Colours:** Shirts — Red and Blue
Limited Company: 1927	Shorts — Blue
Admitted to League: 1932	**Telephone No.:** (0252) 20211
Former Name(s): None	**Ticket Information:** (0252) 20211
Nickname: 'Shots'	**Pitch Size:** 117 x 76yds
Ground: Recreation Ground, High Street,	**Ground Capacity:** 5,000
Aldershot GU11 1TW	**Seating Capacity:** 1,885

GENERAL INFORMATION
Supporters Club Administrator:
D. Bayly
Address: 213 High Street, Aldershot
Telephone Number: (0252) 22233
Car Parking: Parsons Barracks Car Park — adjacent
Coach Parking: Contact local police
Nearest Railway Station: Aldershot (5 minutes walk)
Nearest Bus Station: Aldershot
Club Shop:
Opening Times: Weekdays 9.00-5.00 and Saturday Matchdays 9.30-12.00 and one hour before and after game
Telephone No.: (0252) 311992
Postal Sales: Yes
Nearest Police Station: Wellington Avenue, Aldershot (½ mile)
Police Force: Hampshire Constabulary
Police Telephone Number: (0252) 24545

GROUND INFORMATION
Away Supporters' Entrances: High Street turnstiles/Redan
Away Supporters' Sections: East Bank (covered standing), South Stand, East wing (seated) — available only to members of visiting clubs
Family Facilities: Location of Stand: West Wing of South Stand
Capacity of Stand: 200

DISABLED SUPPORTERS INFORMATION
Wheelchairs: Small number by prior arrangement
Disabled Toilets: None
The Blind: No special facilities

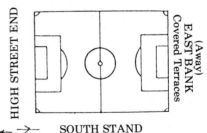

Travelling Supporters Information:
Routes: From East: Take Aldershot signs from Guildford (A323) into High Street, ground on right; From West, South and London: Exit M3 (Junction 4) then A325 to Aldershot, after 5 miles 1st exit at Roundabout into Wellington Avenue, to High Street, ground on left.

ARSENAL FC

Founded: 1886
Turned Professional: 1891
Limited Company: 1893
Admitted to League: 1893
Former Name(s): Royal Arsenal (1886-91);
Woolwich Arsenal (1891-1914)
Nickname: 'Gunners'
Ground: Arsenal Stadium, Avenell
Road, Highbury, London N5 1BU

Record Attendance: 73,295 (9/3/35)
Colours: Shirts — Red with White Sleeves
Shorts — White
Telephone No.: (071) 226-0304
Ticket Information: (071) 359-0131
Pitch Size: 110 x 71yds
Ground Capacity: 41,188
Seating Capacity: 18,140

GENERAL INFORMATION
Supporters Club Administrator: Barry Baker
Address: 154 St. Thomas's Road, Finsbury Park, London N4
Telephone Number: (071) 226-1627
Car Parking: Street Parking
Coach Parking: Drayton Park (N5)
Nearest Railway Station: Drayton Park/Finsbury Park
Nearest Tube Station: Arsenal (Piccadilly) Adjacent
Club Shop:
Opening Times: Weekdays 9.30-5.00
Sat. Matchdays 1.00pm onwards
Telephone No.: (071) 226 9562
Postal Sales: Yes
Nearest Police Station: 284 Hornsey Rd, Holloway
Police Force: Metropolitan
Police Telephone Number: (071) 263-9090

GROUND INFORMATION
Away Supporters' Entrances: Highbury Hill Turnstiles
Away Supporters' Sections: South Terrace (Clock End) — partially covered
Family Facilities: Location of Stand: North Side of West Stand
Capacity of Stand: 800

DISABLED SUPPORTERS INFORMATION
Wheelchairs: Accommodated, Disabled Section Lower Tier East Stand
Disabled Toilets: Yes
The Blind: Commentaries Available

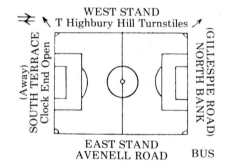

Travelling Supporters Information:
Routes: From North: Exit M1 junction 2 following City signs. After Holloway Road Station (6¼ mls) 3rd left into Drayton Park, after ¾ mile right into Aubert Park and 2nd left into Avenell Road. From South: From London Bridge follow signs to Bank of England then Angel. Right at Traffic-lights to Highbury Roundabout (1 mile), into Holloway Road then 3rd right into Drayton Park (then as North). From West: Exit M4 Junction 1 towards Chiswick (A315), left after 1 mile (A40) to M41 then A40 (m) to A501 Ring Road, turn left at Angel to Highbury Roundabout (then as South).

ASTON VILLA FC

Founded: 1874
Turned Professional: 1885
Limited Company: 1896
Admitted to League: 1888 (Founder)
Former Name(s): None
Nickname: 'The Villans'; 'Villa'
Ground: Villa Park, Trinity Road, Birmingham B6 6HE

Record Attendance: 76,588 (2/3/46)
Colours: Shirts — Claret with Blue Sleeves Shorts — White
Telephone No.: (021) 327-2299
Ticket Information: (021) 327-5353
Pitch Size: 115 x 75yds
Ground Capacity: 40,277
Seating Capacity: 18,069

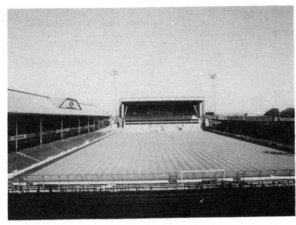

GENERAL INFORMATION
Supporters Club Administrator: —
Address: c/o Club's Commercial Dept.
Telephone Number: (021) 327-5399
Car Parking: Asda Car Park, Aston Hall Road
Coach Parking: Asda Car Park, Aston Hall Road
Nearest Railway Station: Witton
Nearest Bus Station: Birmingham Centre
Club Shop:
Opening Times: Weekdays/Matchdays: 9.30-5.00 (Closes for match)
Telephone No.: (021) 327-2800
Postal Sales: Yes
Nearest Police Station: Queen's Road, Aston (½ mile)
Police Force: West Midlands
Police Telephone Number: (021) 327-6551

GROUND INFORMATION
Away Supporters' Entrances: Standing — Doors R & S, Seating — Doors P & Q
Away Supporters' Sections: Witton End Terracing (Standing) — Witton Lane Stand (Seating)
Family Facilities: Location of Stand: North Stand
Capacity of Stand: 3,940

DISABLED SUPPORTERS INFORMATION
Wheelchairs: Accommodated in special section — Trinity Road Stand
Disabled Toilets: Yes, Trinity Road Stand
The Blind: Commentaries by arrangement

TRINITY ROAD STAND & ENCLOSURE

HOLTE END

(Home) (Away)

WITTON LANE STAND

NORTH STAND (MEMBERS ONLY)

WITTON END TERRACE (AWAY — COVERED)

BUS

Travelling Supporters Information:
Routes: From all parts: Exit M6 Junction 6 (Spaghetti Junction). Follow signs Birmingham (NE), 3rd Exit at Roundabout and in ½ mile, Right into Aston Hall Road.
Bus Services: Service 7 from Corporation Street to Witton Square, also specials.

BARNET FC

Founded: 1888	**Record Attendance:** 11,026 (1952)
Turned Professional:	**Colours:** Shirts — Amber
Limited Company:	Shorts — Black
Admitted to League: 1991	**Telephone No.:** (081) 441 6932
Former Name(s): Barnet Alston	**Ticket Information:** (081) 441 6932
Nickname: 'Bees'	**Pitch Size:** 113 x 73yds
Ground: Underhill Stadium, Barnet Lane,	**Ground Capacity:** 10,000
Barnet, Herts. EN5 2BE	**Seating Capacity:** 1,000

GENERAL INFORMATION
Supporters Club Administrator: Liz Ashfield
Address: 42 Connaught Road, Barnet, Herts
Telephone Number: (081) 440 6625
Car Parking: Street Parking
Coach Parking: By Police Direction
Nearest Railway Station: New Barnet (1½ miles)
Nearest Tube Station: High Barnet (Northern) 5 mins.
Club Shop:
Opening Times: Tuesdays & Thursdays 10.00 — 4.00 & Matchdays 1½ hours before kick-off
Telephone No.: (081) 441 6932
Postal Sales: Yes
Nearest Police Station: Barnet (¼ mile)
Police Force: Metropolitan
Police Telephone Number: (081) 200 2212

GROUND INFORMATION
Away Supporters' Entrances: Priory Grove
Away Supporters' Sections: East Terrace
Family Facilities: Location of Stand: None
Capacity of Stand: —
Away Families: —

DISABLED SUPPORTERS INFORMATION
Wheelchairs: Accommodated — Barnet Lane
Disabled Toilets: None
The Blind: No Special Facilities

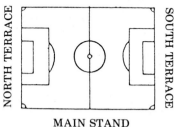

(GREAT NORTH RD)
ENCLOSURE

NORTH TERRACE

SOUTH TERRACE

MAIN STAND
BARNET LANE

Travelling Supporters Information:
Routes: The ground is situated off the Great North Road (A1000) at the foot of Barnet Hill near to the junction with Station Road (A110). Barnet Lane is on to the West of the A1000 next to the cricket ground.

BARNSLEY FC

Founded: 1887	**Record Attendance:** 40,255 (15/2/36)
Turned Professional: 1888	**Colours:** Shirts — Red
Limited Company: 1899	Shorts — White
Admitted to League: 1898	**Telephone No.:** (0226) 295353
Former Name(s): Barnsley St. Peter's	**Ticket Information:** (0226) 295353
Nickname: 'Tykes'; 'Colliers'; 'Reds'	**Pitch Size:** 110 x 75yds
Ground: Oakwell Ground, Grove Street,	**Ground Capacity:** 27,464
Barnsley, S71 1ET	**Seating Capacity:** 2,154

GENERAL INFORMATION
Supporters Club Administrator: Mr. S. Curry
Address: c/o Barnsley FC Social Club, Oakwell Ground, Barnsley
Telephone Number: (0226) 287664
Car Parking: Queen's Ground Car Park (Adjacent)
Coach Parking: Queen's Ground Car Park (Adjacent)
Nearest Railway Station: Barnsley Exchange
Nearest Bus Station: Barnsley
Club Shop:
Opening Times: Weekdays 9.00-5.00; Sat. Matchdays 9.00-5.30
Telephone No.: (0226) 295353
Postal Sales: Yes
Nearest Police Station: Churchfields, Barnsley
Police Force: South Yorkshire
Police Telephone Number: (0226) 206161

GROUND INFORMATION
Away Supporters' Entrances: Spion Kop Turnstiles (Nos 41 to 47)
Away Supporters' Sections: Spion Kop
Family Facilities: Location of Stand: Accommodated throughout
Capacity of Stand: —

DISABLED SUPPORTERS INFORMATION
Wheelchairs: Accommodated in Disabled Stand (also Away Fans)
Disabled Toilets: Yes
The Blind: Commentary for Blind

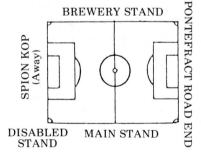

Travelling Supporters Information:
Routes: From All Parts: Exit M1 Junction 37 and follow 'Football Ground' signs to ground (2 miles)

BIRMINGHAM CITY FC

Founded: 1875	**Record Attendance:** 68,844 (11/2/39)
Turned Professional: 1885	**Colours:** Shirts — Blue and White
Limited Company: 1888	Shorts — White
Admitted to League: 1892	**Telephone No.:** (021) 772-0101/2689
Former Name(s): Small Heath Alliance FC	**Ticket Information:** (021) 766-8274
(1875-88); Small Heath FC (1888-1905);	**Pitch Size:** 115 x 75yds
Birmingham FC (1905-45)	**Ground Capacity:** 27,465
Nickname: 'Blues'	**Seating Capacity:** 8,868

Ground: St. Andrew's, St. Andrew's Street, Birmingham B9 4NH

GENERAL INFORMATION
Supporters Club Administrator: Linda Godman
Address: 69 Malmesbury Road, Small Heath, Birmingham
Telephone Number: (021) 773-5088
Car Parking: Coventry Road & Cattell Road Car Parks
Coach Parking: Tilton Road
Nearest Railway Station: Bordesley (5 minutes walk)
Nearest Bus Station: Digbeth
Club Shop:
Opening Times: Weekdays 9.30-4.30; Sat. Matchdays 9.30-6.00
Telephone No.: (021) 766-8274
Postal Sales: Yes
Nearest Police Station: Bordesley Green (½ mile)
Police Force: West Midlands
Police Telephone Number: (021) 772-1166

GROUND INFORMATION
Away Supporters' Entrances: Entrance 'J' Tilton Road
Away Supporters' Sections: Tilton Road End
Family Facilities: Location of Stand: City End
Capacity of Stand: 2,343

DISABLED SUPPORTERS INFORMATION
Wheelchairs: Limited to Pass Holders (Away fans by prior arrangement)
Disabled Toilets: None
The Blind: No Special Facilities

Travelling Supporters Information:
Routes: From All Parts: Exit M6 Junction 6, to A38(M) (Aston Expressway), leave at 2nd exit then 1st exit at Roundabout along Dartmouth Middleway, after 1¼ miles take left into St. Andrew's Street.
Bus Services: Service 97 from Birmingham; Services 98 & 99 from Digbeth.

BLACKBURN ROVERS FC

Founded: 1875	**Record Attendance:** 61,783 (2/3/29)
Turned Professional: 1880	**Colours:** Shirts — Blue & White Halves
Limited Company: 1897	Shorts — White
Admitted to League: 1888 (Founder)	**Telephone No.:** (0254) 55432
Former Name(s): Blackburn Grammar	**Ticket Information:** (0254) 55432
School Old Boys FC	**Pitch Size:** 117 x 73yds
Nickname: 'Rovers' 'Blues & Whites'	**Ground Capacity:** 17,819
Ground: Ewood Park, Blackburn,	**Seating Capacity:** 2,989
Lancashire, BB2 4JF	

GENERAL INFORMATION
Supporters Club Administrator: Barbara Magee
Address: c/o Club
Telephone Number: (0254) 55432
Car Parking: Street Parking (nearby)
Coach Parking: By Police direction
Nearest Railway Station: Blackburn Central (1½ miles)
Nearest Bus Station: Blackburn Central (1½ miles)
Club Shop:
Opening Times: Weekdays 9.00-5.00
Matchdays 1.00-5.30
Telephone No.: (0254) 61272
Postal Sales: Yes
Nearest Police Station: Blackburn (2 miles)
Police Force: Lancashire
Police Telephone Number: (0254) 51212

GROUND INFORMATION
Away Supporters' Entrances: Darwen End Turnstiles
Away Supporters' Sections: Darwen End (mostly covered)
Family Facilities: Location of Stand: In Walkersteel Stand
Capacity of Stand: Approx. 629

DISABLED SUPPORTERS INFORMATION
Wheelchairs: Disabled Section in Walkersteel Stand
Disabled Toilets: In Disabled Section
The Blind: Commentary available by arrangement

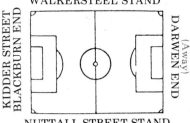

RIVERSIDE LANE
WALKERSTEEL STAND
KIDDER STREET
BLACKBURN END
DARWEN END
(Away)
NUTTALL STREET STAND
BOLTON ROAD

Travelling Supporters Information:
Routes: From North, South and West: Exit M6 Junction 31, or take A666, follow signs for Blackburn then for Bolton Road, after 1½ miles turn left into Kidder St.; From East: Use A679 or A677 and follow signs for Bolton Rd (then as above)

BLACKPOOL FC

Founded: 1887	**Record Attendance:** 38,098 (17/9/55)
Turned Professional: 1887	**Colours:** Shirts — Tangerine
Limited Company: 1896	Shorts — White
Admitted to League: 1896	**Telephone No.:** (0253) 404331
Former Name(s): Merged with Blackpool	**Ticket Information:** (0253) 404331
St. Johns 1887	**Pitch Size:** 111 x 73yds
Nickname: 'Seasiders'	**Ground Capacity:** 9,641
Ground: Bloomfield Road, Blackpool	**Seating Capacity:** 3,196
Lancashire FY1 6JJ	

GENERAL INFORMATION

Supporters Club Administrator: Mr. F. Butcher
Address: Blackpool Supporters' Club, Bloomfield Road, Blackpool
Telephone Number: (0253) 46428 (evenings only 7pm-11pm)
Car Parking: Car Park at Ground (3,000 cars) and Street Parking
Coach Parking: Mecca Car Park (behind Spion Kop)
Nearest Railway Station: Blackpool South (5 mins. walk)
Nearest Bus Station: Talbot Rd (2 miles)
Club Shop:
Opening Times: Daily 9.00-5.00
Telephone No.: (0253) 404331
Postal Sales: Yes
Nearest Police Station: South Shore, Waterloo Road, Blackpool
Police Force: Lancashire
Police Telephone Number: (0253) 293933

GROUND INFORMATION

Away Supporters' Entrances: Spion Kop Turnstiles
Away Supporters' Sections: Spion Kop (Open) & East Paddock North Section (Covered)
Family Facilities: Location of Stand: West Stand (South end)
Capacity of Stand: 400 (Family area)

DISABLED SUPPORTERS INFORMATION

Wheelchairs: Accommodated
Disabled Toilets: None
The Blind: Headphone commentaries (South Stand)

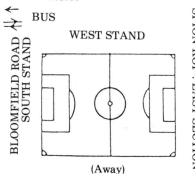

Travelling Supporters Information:

Routes: From All Parts: Exit M6 Junction 32 to M55. Follow signs for main car parks along new 'spine' road to car parks at side of ground.

BOLTON WANDERERS FC

Founded: 1874
Turned Professional: 1880
Limited Company: 1895
Admitted to League: 1888 (Founder)
Former Name(s): Christchurch FC (1874-1877)
Nickname: 'Trotters'
Ground: Burnden Park, Manchester Road, Bolton BL3 2QR

Record Attendance: 69,912 (18/2/33)
Colours: Shirts — White
Shorts — Blue
Telephone No.: (0204) 389200
Ticket Information: (0204) 21101
Pitch Size: 113 x 75yds
Ground Capacity: 25,000
Seating Capacity: 8,000

GENERAL INFORMATION
Supporters Club Administrator: None
Address: —
Telephone Number: —
Car Parking: Rosehill Car Park (Nearby)
Coach Parking: Rosehill Car Park, Manchester Road
Nearest Railway Station: Bolton Trinity Street (½ mile)
Nearest Bus Station: Moor Lane, Bolton
Club Shop:
Opening Times: Daily 9.30-5.30
Telephone No.: (0204) 389200
Postal Sales: Yes
Nearest Police Station: Howell Croft, Bolton
Police Force: Greater Manchester
Police Telephone Number: (0204) 22466

GROUND INFORMATION
Away Supporters' Entrances: Embankment Turnstiles
Away Supporters' Sections: Embankment (Open) & Covered Seating
Family Facilities: Location of Stand: Greater Lever Stand
Capacity of Stand: 3,000

DISABLED SUPPORTERS INFORMATION
Wheelchairs: Accommodated
Disabled Toilets: None
The Blind: No Special Facilities

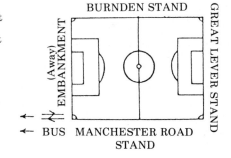

Travelling Supporters Information:
Routes: From North: Exit M61 Junction 5 or use A666 or A676. Follow signs for Farnworth (B653) into Manchester Road. After ½ mile turn left into Croft Lane; From South, East and West: Exit M62 Junction 14 to M61, after 2 miles leave motorway then 1st exit at Roundabout (B6536). After 2 miles turn right into Croft Lane.

AFC BOURNEMOUTH

Founded: 1890
Turned Professional: 1912
Limited Company: 1914
Admitted to League: 1923
Former Name(s): Boscombe St. Johns FC
(1890-9); Boscombe FC (1899-1923);
Bournemouth & Boscombe Ath FC
(1923-72)
Nickname: 'Cherries'

Record Attendance: 28,799 (2/3/57)
Colours: Shirts — Red and White Striped
Shorts — White
Telephone No.: (0202) 395381
Ticket Information: (0202) 395381
Pitch Size: 112 x 75yds
Ground Capacity: 11,375
Seating Capacity: 3,958

Ground: Dean Court, Bournemouth, Dorset BH7 7AF

GENERAL INFORMATION
Supporters Club Administrator: Dean
Court Supporters' Club
Address: Bournemouth BH7 7AF
Telephone Number: (0202) 398313
Car Parking: Car Park (1500 cars)
Behind Main Stand
Coach Parking: Kings Park (Nearby)
Nearest Railway Station:
Bournemouth Central (1½ miles)
Nearest Bus Station: Holdenhurst Rd.,
Bournemouth
Club Shop:
Opening Times: Weekdays 9.00-5.00
Sat. Matchdays 1.00-6.00
Telephone No.: (0202) 397777
Postal Sales: Yes
Nearest Police Station: Boscombe (¼
mile)
Police Force: Dorset
Police Telephone Number: (0202)
22099

GROUND INFORMATION
Away Supporters' Entrances: Main Stand
Turnstiles (Block A)
Away Supporters' Sections: Brighton Beach
Terrace (open)
Family Facilities: Location of Stand:
Family Block (Main Stand)
Capacity of Stand: 700

DISABLED SUPPORTERS INFORMATION
Wheelchairs: Accommodated by prior arrange-
ment — in front of South Stand (covered
shelter)
Disabled Toilets: Yes
The Blind: No facilities

Travelling Supporters Information:
Routes: From North & East: Take A338 into Bournemouth and turn left at 'Kings Park' turning.
Then first left at mini-roundabout and first right into Thistlebarrow Road for Ground. From
West: Use A3049, turning right at Wallisdown Roundabout to Talbot Roundabout. Take first
exit at Talbot Roundabout (over Wessex Way), then left at mini-roundabout. Go straight across
traffic lights then right at mini-roundabout into Kings Park for ground.
Bus Services: Service 25 passes ground.

BRADFORD CITY FC

Founded: 1903	**Record Attendance:** 39,146 (11/3/11)
Turned Professional: 1903	**Colours:** Shirts — Claret and Amber
Limited Company: 1908 (Reformed 1983)	**Stripes Shorts** — Claret
Admitted to League: 1903	**Telephone No.:** (0274) 306062
Former Name(s): None	**Ticket Information:** (0274) 307050
Nickname: 'Bantams'	**Pitch Size:** 110 x 80yds
Ground: Valley Parade, Bradford,	**Ground Capacity:** 14,810
BD8 7OY	**Seating Capacity:** 6,500

GENERAL INFORMATION
Supporters Club Administrator: M. Neale
Address: 10 Rossfield Road, Bradford 9
Telephone Number: (0274) 545642
Car Parking: Street parking and car parks (£2 entry charge)
Coach Parking: By Police direction
Nearest Railway Station: Bradford Interchange
Nearest Bus Station: Bradford Interchange
Club Shop:
Opening Times: Monday to Saturday 10.00 a.m. — 5.00 p.m.
Telephone No.: (0274) 306062
Postal Sales: Yes
Nearest Police Station: Tyrrells, Bradford
Police Force: West Yorkshire
Police Telephone Number: (0274) 723422

GROUND INFORMATION
Away Supporters' Entrances: Midland Road
Away Supporters' Sections: Midland Road Side
Family Facilities: Location of Stand:
T & A Family Stand
Capacity of Stand: 2,000 seated

DISABLED SUPPORTERS INFORMATION
Wheelchairs: Accommodation for 20 wheelchairs
Disabled Toilets: None
The Blind: No special facilities

Travelling Supporters Information:
Routes: From North: Take A650 and follow signs for Bradford. A third of a mile after junction with Ring Road turn left into Valley Parade. From East, South and West: Take M62 and exit Junction 26 onto M606. At end take 2nd left from roundabout and onto A6177 Ring Road. At next roundabout (3rd exit) turn right to City Centre (A614). At second roundabout turn right onto Central Ring Road (A6181) the left at next roundabout and left again at following roundabout marked 'Local Access Only'. Pass through traffic lights at the top of the hill following Keighley (A650) sign. Ground is then ½ mile along on the right.

BRENTFORD FC

Founded: 1889	**Record Attendance:** 39,626 (5/3/38)
Turned Professional: 1899	**Colours:** Shirts — Red & White Stripes
Limited Company: 1901	Shorts — Black
Admitted to League: 1920	**Telephone No.:** (081) 847-2511
Former Name(s): None	**Ticket Information:** (081) 847-2511
Nickname: 'Bees'	**Pitch Size:** 110 x 74yds
Ground: Griffin Park, Braemar Road,	**Ground Capacity:** 11,100
Brentford, Middlesex TW8 ONT	**Seating Capacity:** 3,500

GENERAL INFORMATION
Supporters Club Administrator:
Mr. P. Gilham
Address: 16 Hartland Road, Hampton Hill, Middx.
Telephone Number: (081) 941-0425
Car Parking: Street Parking
Coach Parking: Layton Road Car Park
Nearest Railway Station: Brentford Central
Nearest Tube Station: South Ealing (Piccadilly)
Club Shop:
Opening Times: Matchdays only (Weekdays telephone club)
Telephone No.: (081) 560-2021
Postal Sales: Yes
Nearest Police Station: Brentford
Police Force: Metropolitan
Police Telephone Number: (081) 577-1212

GROUND INFORMATION
Away Supporters' Entrances: Ealing Road Turnstiles
Away Supporters' Sections: Ealing Road End (Open) — Covered accommodation in wet weather
Family Facilities: Location of Stand: Brook Road End
Capacity of Stand: 600

DISABLED SUPPORTERS INFORMATION
Wheelchairs: Accommodated in Disabled Section — Brook Road End
Disabled Toilets: Yes
The Blind: Commentaries in Braemar Road Stand

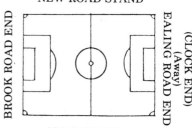

Travelling Supporters Information:
Routes: From North & East: Take A406 North Circular (from M1/A1) to Chiswick. Follow South Circular signs for ¼ mile then turn right A315. After ½ mile turn right into Ealing Road. From West: Exit M4 Junction 2, U-turn at lights (legal), take A4 heading West. In ½ mile turn left into Ealing Road. From South: Use A3/M3/A240 or A316 to Junction South Circular (A205) over Kew Bridge turn left on to A315 turn right (½ mile) into Ealing Road.

BRIGHTON & HOVE ALBION FC

Founded: 1900	**Record Attendance:** 36,747 (27/12/58)
Turned Professional: 1900	**Colours:** Shirts — Blue & White Stripes
Limited Company: 1904	Shorts — Blue
Admitted to League: 1920	**Telephone No.:** (0273) 739535
Former Name(s): Brighton & Hove	**Ticket Information:** (0273) 739535
Rangers FC (1900-01)	**Pitch Size:** 112 x 75yds
Nickname: 'Seagulls'	**Ground Capacity:** 18,493
Ground: Goldstone Ground, Old Shoreham	**Seating Capacity:** 5,228
Road, Hove, Sussex, BN3 7DE	

GENERAL INFORMATION
Supporters Club Administrator: Sue Huffer
Address: 8 Frant Road, Hove, BN3 7QS
Telephone Number: c/o (0273) 739535
Car Parking: Greyhound Stadium and street parking
Coach Parking: Conway Street, Hove
Nearest Railway Station: Hove (5 mins walk)
Nearest Bus Station: Brighton Pool Valley
Club Shop: Sports Express, Newtown Road
Opening Times: Weekdays 9.00-5.00
Telephone No.: (0273) 26412
Postal Sales: Yes
Nearest Police Station: Hove (1 mile)
Police Force: Sussex
Police Telephone Number: (0273) 778922

GROUND INFORMATION
Away Supporters' Entrances: Goldstone Lane Turnstiles
Away Supporters' Sections: South East Corner (Open Terrace); South Stand (Seats)
Family Facilities: Location of Stand: South Stand — Entrance Newtown Road
Capacity of Stand: 1,500

DISABLED SUPPORTERS INFORMATION
Wheelchairs: Accommodated in Disabled Section (SW Corner)
Disabled Toilets: Yes
The Blind: Commentaries in West Stand

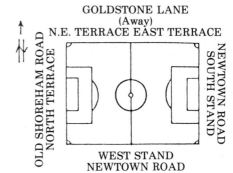

GOLDSTONE LANE
(Away)
N.E. TERRACE   EAST TERRACE
OLD SHOREHAM ROAD
NORTH TERRACE
NEWTOWN ROAD
SOUTH STAND
WEST STAND
NEWTOWN ROAD

Travelling Supporters Information:
Routes: From North: Take A23, turn right 2 miles after Pyecombe follow Hove signs for 1 mile, bear left into Nevill Road (A2023), then turn left at Crossroads (1 mile), into Old Shoreham Road; From East: Take A27 to Brighton then follow Worthing signs into Old Shoreham Road; From West: Take A27 straight into Old Shoreham Road.
Bus Services: Service 11 passes ground.

BRISTOL CITY FC

<table>
<tr><td>

Founded: 1894
Turned Professional: 1897
Limited Company: 1897
Admitted to League: 1901
Former Name(s): Bristol South End FC (1894-7)
Nickname: 'Robins'
Ground: Ashton Gate, Winterstoke Road, Ashton Road, Bristol BS3 2EJ

</td><td>

Record Attendance: 43,335 (16/2/35)
Colours: Shirts — Red
Shorts — White
Telephone No.: (0272) 632812
Ticket Information: (0272) 632812
Pitch Size: 120 x 75yds
Ground Capacity: 25,271
Seating Capacity: 16,000

</td></tr>
</table>

GENERAL INFORMATION
Supporters Club Administrator: Mr. G. Williams
Address: c/o Club
Telephone Number: (0272) 665554
Car Parking: Street Parking
Coach Parking: Cannon's March
Nearest Railway Station: Bristol Temple Meads (1½ miles)
Nearest Bus Station: Bristol City Centre
Club Shop:
Opening Times: Weekdays 9.00-5.00 & Matchdays
Telephone No.: (0272) 632812
Postal Sales: Yes
Nearest Police Station: Kings Mead Lane (2 miles) — office at ground
Police Force: Avon/Somerset
Police Telephone Number: (0272) 277777

GROUND INFORMATION
Away Supporters' Entrances: Ashton Road — Turnstiles 51-57
Away Supporters' Sections: Ashton Road — Open End
Family Facilities: Location of Stand: Dolman Stand
Capacity of Stand: 4,741

DISABLED SUPPORTERS INFORMATION
Wheelchairs: Accommodated at Pitch Side
Disabled Toilets: Yes
The Blind: Commentary available

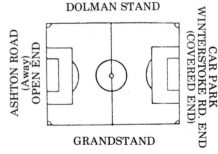

Travelling Supporters Information:
Routes: From North & West: Exit M5 Junction 16, take A38 to Bristol City centre and follow A38 Taunton signs. Cross Swing Bridge (1¼ mile) and bear left into Winterstoke Road; From East: Take M4 then M32 follow signs to city centre (then as North & West); From South: Exit M5 Junction 18 and follow Taunton signs over Swing Bridge (then as above).
Bus Services: Service 51 from Railway Station

BRISTOL ROVERS FC

Founded: 1883	**Record Attendance:** 18,000
Turned Professional: 1897	**Colours:** Shirts — Blue & White Quarters
Limited Company: 1896	Shorts — White
Admitted to League: 1920	**Telephone No.:** (0272) 352508
Former Name(s): Black Arabs FC 1883-84	**Ticket Information:** (0272) 352508
Eastville Rovers FC (1884-96), Bristol	**Pitch Size:** 110 x 76yds
Eastville Rovers FC (1896-7)	**Ground Capacity:** 9,813
Nickname: 'Pirates'; 'Rovers'	**Seating Capacity:** 652
Ground: Twerton Park, Bath, Avon	**Office:** 199 Two Mile Hill Rd., Kingswood
	Bristol BS15, 7AZ

GENERAL INFORMATION
Supporters Club Administrator: Mr. Steve Burns
Address: c/o Club's Office
Telephone Number: (0272) 510363
Car Parking: Very little space at ground
Coach Parking: Avon Street, Bath
Nearest Railway Station: Bath Spa (1½ miles)
Nearest Bus Station: Avon Street, Bath
Club Shop:
Opening Times: Weekdays (club offices) 9.00-5.00 p.m.
Telephone No.: (0272) 352508
Postal Sales: Yes
Nearest Police Station: Bath (1½ miles)
Police Force: Avon & Somerset
Police Telephone Number: (0225) 444343

GROUND INFORMATION
Away Supporters' Entrances: Bristol End
Away Supporters' Sections: Bristol End
Family Facilities: Location of Stand:
Family Enclosure Terrace — Bath End
New Family Stand at side of Main Stand —
Opening December 1991
Capacity of Stand: 652

DISABLED SUPPORTERS INFORMATION
Wheelchairs: Accommodated Family Stand
Disabled Toilets: Family Stand (Dec. 1991)
The Blind: Commentaries by arrangement

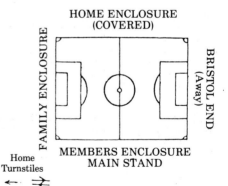

Travelling Supporters Information:
Routes: Take the A36 into Bath city centre. Follow along Pulteney Road, then right into Claverton Street and along Lower Bristol Road (A36). Left under railway (1½ miles) into Twerton High Street and ground on left.

BURNLEY FC

Founded: 1882	**Record Attendance:** 54,775 (23/2/24)
Turned Professional: 1883	**Colours:** Shirts — Claret with Blue sleeves
Limited Company: 1897	Shorts — White
Admitted to League: 1888 (Founder)	**Telephone No.:** (0282) 27777
Former Name(s): Burnley Rovers FC	**Ticket Information:** (0282) 27777
Nickname: 'Clarets'	**Pitch Size:** 115 x 73yds
Ground: Turf Moor, Brunshaw Road,	**Ground Capacity:** 20,912
Burnley, Lancs, BB10 4BX	**Seating Capacity:** 7,437

GENERAL INFORMATION
Supporters Club Administrator: David Spencer
Address: c/o Club
Telephone Number: (0282) 35176
Car Parking: Church Street & Fulledge Rec. Car Parks (5 minutes walk)
Coach Parking: By Police direction
Nearest Railway Station: Burnley Central (1½ miles)
Nearest Bus Station: Burnley (5 minutes walk)
Club Shop:
Opening Times: Office Hours
Telephone No.: (0282) 27777
Postal Sales: Yes
Nearest Police Station: Parker Lane, Burnley (5 minutes walk)
Police Force: Lancashire
Police Telephone Number: (0282) 25001

GROUND INFORMATION
Away Supporters' Entrances: Belvedere Road turnstiles
Away Supporters' Sections: Covered Terracing
Family Facilities: Location of Stand:
Cricket Field Stand (Members only)
Capacity of Stand: 4,276
Away Families: None

DISABLED SUPPORTERS INFORMATION
Wheelchairs: Accommodated in front of Bob Lord Stand
Disabled Toilets: None
The Blind: No special facilities

Travelling Supporters Information:
Routes: From North: Follow A56 to Town Centre and take 1st exit at roundabout into Yorkshire Street. Follow over crossroads into Brunshaw Road; From East: Follow A646 to A671 then along Todmorden Road to Town Centre. Follow down until crossroads and turn right into Brunshaw Road; From West & South: Exit M6 Junction 31, taking Blackburn bypass & A679 into Town Centre, 3rd exit from roundabout into Yorkshire Street (then as North).

BURY FC

Founded: 1885	**Record Attendance:** 35,000 (9/1/60)
Turned Professional: 1885	**Colours:** Shirts — White
Limited Company: 1897	Shorts — Navy
Admitted to League: 1894	**Telephone No.:** (061) 764 4881/2
Former Name(s): None	**Ticket Information:** (061) 764 4881/2
Nickname: 'Shakers'	**Pitch Size:** 112 x 72yds
Ground: Gigg Lane, Bury, Lancs	**Ground Capacity:** 8,000
BL9 9HR	**Seating Capacity:** 2,500

GENERAL INFORMATION
Supporters Club Administrator:
Address: c/o Club
Telephone Number: (061) 764 4881
Car Parking: Street Parking
Coach Parking: By Police Direction
Nearest Railway Station: Bury Metro Interchange (1 mile)
Nearest Bus Station: Bury Metro Interchange (1 mile)
Club Shop:
Opening Times: Daily 9.00-5.00
Telephone No.: (061) 705 2144
Postal Sales: Yes (Price lists available)
Nearest Police Station: Irwell Street, Bury
Police Force: Greater Manchester
Police Telephone Number: (061) 872 5050

GROUND INFORMATION
Away Supporters' Entrances: Gigg Lane
Away Supporters' Sections: Cemetery End Covered Terracing/B. Stand Seating
Family Facilities: Location of Stand: Main Stand — 'A' Stand
Capacity of Stand: 500
Away Families: None

DISABLED SUPPORTERS INFORMATION
Wheelchairs: Accommodated between Cemetery End and South Stand
Disabled Toilets: None (May be available 1991/92 season)
The Blind: No special facilities

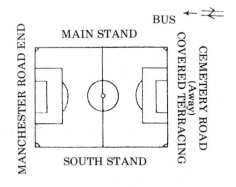

Travelling Supporters Information:
Routes: From North: Exit M66 Junction 2, take Bury Road (A58) for ½ mile, then turn left into Heywood Street and follow this into Parkhills Road until its end, turn left into Manchester Road (A56) then left into Gigg Lane. From South, East & West: M62 Junction 17, take Bury Road (A56) for 3 miles then turn into Gigg Lane.

CAMBRIDGE UNITED FC

Founded: 1919	**Record Attendance:** 14,000 (1/5/70)
Turned Professional: 1946	**Colours:** Shirts — Yellow
Limited Company: 1948	Shorts — Yellow
Admitted to League: 1970	**Telephone No.:** (0223) 241237
Former Name(s): Abbey Utd. FC (1919-49)	**Ticket Information:** (0223) 241237
Nickname: 'U's', 'United'	**Pitch Size:** 110 x 74yds
Ground: Abbey Stadium, Newmarket	**Ground Capacity:** 9,998
Road, Cambridge CB5 8LL	**Seating Capacity:** 3,410

GENERAL INFORMATION
Supporters Club Administrator: —
Address: c/o The Club
Telephone Number: —
Car Parking: Coldhams Common
Coach Parking: Coldhams Common
Nearest Railway Station: Cambridge (2 miles)
Nearest Bus Station: Cambridge City Centre
Club Shop:
Opening Times: Weekdays 10.00-5.00 & matchdays
Telephone No.: (0223) 241237
Postal Sales: Yes
Nearest Police Station: Parkside, Cambridge
Police Force: Cambridgeshire
Police Telephone Number: (0223) 358966

GROUND INFORMATION
Away Supporters' Entrances: Coldham Common — Turnstiles 16-19
Away Supporters' Sections: Allotment End (part covered — 360 seats/1,900 standing)
Family Facilities: Location of Stand: Main Stand
Capacity of Stand: 60
Away Families: By prior arrangement

DISABLED SUPPORTERS INFORMATION
Wheelchairs: Accommodated in Disabled section — in front of Main Stand
Disabled Toilets: None
The Blind: No Special facilities

Travelling Supporters Information:
Routes: From North: Take A1 and A604 into City Centre, then A45 Newmarket signs into Newmarket Road; From East: Take A45 straight into Newmarket Road; From South: Take A10 or A130 into City Centre (then as North); From West: Take A422 into Cambridge and pick up A45 into Newmarket Road.
Bus Services: Service 180 & 181 from Railway Station to City Centre/182 & 183 to Ground.

CARDIFF CITY FC

Founded: 1899
Turned Professional: 1910
Limited Company: 1910
Admitted to League: 1920
Former Name(s): Riverside FC (1899-1910)
Nickname: 'Bluebirds'
Ground: Ninian Park, Sloper Road
Cardiff, CF1 8SX

Record Attendance: 61,566 (14/10/61)
Colours: Shirts — Blue
Shorts — White
Telephone No.: (0222) 398636
Ticket Information: (0222) 398636
Pitch Size: 112 x 76yds
Ground Capacity: 19,300
Seating Capacity: 3,271

GENERAL INFORMATION

Supporters Club Administrator: Mr. M. Lambert
Address: 2 Station Villas, Llwyd-Coed, Aberdare, M. Glam.
Telephone Number: (0685) 881006
Car Parking: Sloper Road & Street parking
Coach Parking: Sloper Road (Adjacent)
Nearest Railway Station: Cardiff Central (1 miles)
Nearest Bus Station: Cardiff Central
Club Shop:
Opening Times: Weekdays 9.00-5.00 & Matchdays 1½ hours before kick-off
Telephone No.: (0222) 220516
Postal Sales: Yes
Nearest Police Station: Cowbridge Road East, Cardiff (1 mile)
Police Force: South Wales
Police Telephone Number: (0222) 222111

GROUND INFORMATION

Away Supporters' Entrances: Grangetown End, Sloper Road
Away Supporters' Sections: Grangetown End (Open)
Family Facilities: Location of Stand: Below Grandstand and Canton Stand
Capacity of Stand: 3,271
Away Families: None

DISABLED SUPPORTERS INFORMATION

Wheelchairs: Accommodated in Canton Stand/Popular Bank corner
Disabled Toilets: None
The Blind: No Special facilities

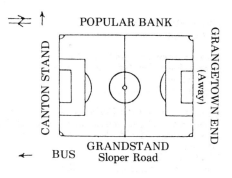

Travelling Supporters Information:

Routes: From North: Take A470 until Junction with Cardiff Bypass. Then 3rd exit at Roundabout A48 to Port Talbot, after 2 miles take 1st exit at Roundabout A4161 (Cowbridge Road). Turn right (½ mile), Lansdowne Road to Crossroads, turn right into Leckwith Road, then turn left (¼ mile) into Sloper Road: From East: Exit M4 taking A48 to Cardiff Bypass (then as North); From West: Take A4161 Cowbridge Road (then as North).
Bus Services: Service No.2 — City Centre to Ground and Service No.1

CARLISLE UNITED FC

Founded: 1903	**Record Attendance:** 27,500 (5/1/57)
Turned Professional: 1903	**Colours:** Shirts — Royal Blue
Limited Company: 1921	Shorts — White
Admitted to League: 1928	**Telephone No.:** (0228) 26237
Former Name(s): Formed by Amalgamation of Shaddongate United FC & Carlisle Red Rose FC	**Ticket Information:** (0228) 26237
	Pitch Size: 117 x 78yds
Nickname: 'Cumbrians' 'Blues'	**Ground Capacity:** 18,506
	Seating Capacity: 2,162

Ground: Brunton Park, Warwick Road, Carlisle CA1 1LL

GENERAL INFORMATION
Supporters Club Administrator: Colin Barton
Address: 6 Old Post Office Court, Devonshire Street, Carlisle
Telephone Number: (0228) 21261
Car Parking: Rear of Ground via St. Aidans Road
Coach Parking: St. Aidans Road Car Park
Nearest Railway Station: Carlisle Citadel (1 mile)
Nearest Bus Station: Lowther Street, Carlisle
Club Shop:
Opening Times: Weekdays 9.00-5.00 Saturdays 10.00-12.00
Telephone No.: (0228) 24014
Postal Sales: Yes
Nearest Police Station: Rickergate, Carlisle (1½ miles)
Police Force: Cumbria Constabulary
Police Telephone Number: (0228) 28191

GROUND INFORMATION
Away Supporters' Entrances: Turnstiles 22 to 25
Away Supporters' Sections: Visitors enclosure
Family Facilities: Location of Stand: Main Stand
Capacity of Stand: 2,162

DISABLED SUPPORTERS INFORMATION
Wheelchairs: Accommodated in Disabled Section (in front of Paddock) by prior arrangement (limited)
Disabled Toilets: None
The Blind: Commentaries available

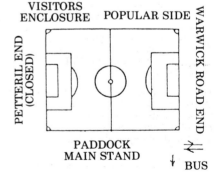

VISITORS ENCLOSURE POPULAR SIDE
PETTERIL END (CLOSED)
WARWICK ROAD END
PADDOCK MAIN STAND
BUS

Travelling Supporters Information:
Routes: From North, South & East: Exit M6 Junction 43 and follow signs for Carlisle (A69) into Warwick Road. From West: Take A69 straight into Warwick Road.

CHARLTON ATHLETIC FC

<table>
<tr><td>

Founded: 1905
Turned Professional: 1920
Limited Company: 1984
Admitted to League: 1921
Former Name(s): None
Nickname: 'Valiants'
Ground: The Valley, Floyd Road, Charlton
London SE7 8BL

</td><td>

Record Attendance: 75,031 (12/2/38)
Colours: Shirts — Red
Shorts — White
Telephone No.: (081) 293 4567
Ticket Information: (081) 293 4567
Pitch Size: 113 x 78yds
Ground Capacity: 12,000
Seating Capacity: 9,000

</td></tr>
</table>

GENERAL INFORMATION
Supporters Club Administrator: Bill Treadgold
Address: 8 Hazel Walk, Bromley, Kent
Telephone Number: 0 1 467 7623
Car Parking: Street Parking
Coach Parking: By Police Direction
Nearest Railway Station: Charlton (2 mins walk)
Nearest Bus Station:
Club Shop:
Opening Times: Weekdays 9.00 - 5.00 p.m. Saturday 9.00-12.00
Telephone No.: 081 293 4567
Postal Sales: Yes
Nearest Police Station: Greenwich (2 miles)
Police Force: Metropolitan
Police Telephone Number: 081 853 8212

BUS

GROUND INFORMATION
Away Supporters' Entrances: Valley Grove
Away Supporters' Sections: South Stand
Family Facilities: Location of Stand:
West Stand
Capacity of Stand: 1,000

DISABLED SUPPORTERS INFORMATION
Wheelchairs: Accommodated
Disabled Toilets: To be built
The Blind: No special facilities

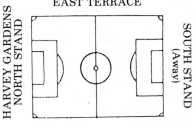

EAST TERRACE

HARVEY GARDENS NORTH STAND

SOUTH STAND (Away)

WEST STAND — VALLEY GROVE

Travelling Supporters Information:
Routes: From North: Follow city signs from A1/M1, then signs for Shoreditch & Whitechapel to A13. Follow Tilbury signs and use Blackwall Tunnel to A102M. Branch left after 1 mile and turn left at T junction into A206. Turn right ½ mile into Charlton Church Lane, then left into Floyd Road; From East: Take A2 to Eltham for Blackwall Tunnel (then as North); From South: Take A21 & A20 to Blackwall Tunnel (then as above); From West: Take M4, then A4 to Central London then signs to Westminster & Embankment — Take A2 Dover Road then A206 (Woolwich). Turn right into Charlton Church Lane, then left into Floyd Road.
Bus Services: Services 53, 54, 75, 177 & 180 from City.

CHELSEA FC

Founded: 1905	**Record Attendance:** 82,905 (12/10/35)
Turned Professional: 1905	**Colours:** Shirts — Blue
Limited Company: 1905	Shorts — Blue
Admitted to League: 1905	**Telephone No.:** (071) 385 5545
Former Name(s): None	**Pitch Size:** 114 x 71yds
Nickname: 'Blues'	**Ground Capacity:** 36,000
Ground: Stamford Bridge, Fulham Road, London SW6 1HS	**Seating Capacity:** 19,100

GENERAL INFORMATION
Supporters Club Administrator: Contact via club
Address: —
Telephone Number:
Car Parking: Street Parking
Coach Parking: By Police Direction
Nearest Railway Station: Fulham Broadway
Nearest Tube Station: Fulham Broadway (District)
Club Shop:
Opening Times: Weekdays 10.30-4.30 & Matchdays
Telephone No.: (071) 381 6172
Postal Sales: Yes
Nearest Police Station: Fulham
Police Force: Metropolitan
Police Telephone Number: (071) 385 1212

GROUND INFORMATION
Away Supporters' Entrances: Brittania Gate
Away Supporters' Sections: North Terrace (Open)
Family Facilities: Location of Stand: East Stand (North Side)
Capacity of Stand: 1,700

DISABLED SUPPORTERS INFORMATION
Wheelchairs: Limited Number Accommodated. (East Stand concourse)
Disabled Toilets: East Stand concourse
The Blind: No special facilities

Travelling Supporters Information:
Routes: From North & East: Follow Central London signs from A1/M1 to Hyde Park Corner, then signs Guildford (A3) to Knightsbridge (A4) after 1 mile turn left into Fulham Road; From South: Take A13 or A24, then A219 to cross Putney Bridge and follow signs 'West End' (A304) to join A308 into Fulham Road; From West: Take M4 then A4 to Central London, then signs to Westminster (A3220). After ¾ mile turn right at crossroads into Fulham Road.

CHESTER CITY FC

Founded: 1884	**Record Attendance:** 20,500 (16/1/52)
Turned Professional: 1902	**Colours:** Shirts — Blue with White pin-
Limited Company: 1909	stripes Shorts — White
Admitted to League: 1931	**Telephone No.:** (0244) 371376
Former Name(s): Chester FC	**Ticket Information:** (0244) 373829
Nickname: 'Blues', 'City'	**Pitch Size:** 114 x 76yds
Office: The Stadium, Sealand Road,	**Ground Capacity:** 10,000
Chester, CH1 4LW	**Seating Capacity:** 535

Ground: Moss Rose Ground, London Road, Macclesfield, Cheshire

GENERAL INFORMATION
Supporters Club Administrator:
B. Hipkiss
Address: c/o Club
Telephone Number: (0244) 371376
Car Parking: Ample near ground
Coach Parking: Near ground
Nearest Railway Station: Macclesfield (1 ml)
Nearest Bus Station: Macclesfield
Club Shop:
Opening Times: No information
Telephone No.: (0244) 378162
Postal Sales: Yes
Nearest Police Station: Macclesfield
Police Force: Cheshire
Police Telephone Number:
Note: Chester City have sold their ground and are sharing with Macclesfield Town until a new ground is built. Correspondence should be sent to the Sealand Road ground in the meantime.

GROUND INFORMATION
Away Supporters' Entrances: Star Lane
Away Supporters' Sections: Star Lane
Family Facilities: Location of Stand:
Family Enclosure
Capacity of Stand: 535
Away Families: None

DISABLED SUPPORTERS INFORMATION
Wheelchairs: Accommodated
Disabled Toilets: None
The Blind: No special facilities

FAMILY ENCLOSURE

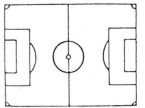

Travelling Supporters Information:
Routes: Exit M6 Junction 18. Eastwards on A54, then A535 to Chelford. Turn right on to A537 to Macclesfield. Turn right from Chester Road into Crompton Road, then go left at the end along Park Lane (A536), and Park Street. Turn right into Mill Lane (A523 for Leek), then take Cross Street and London Road. Ground on left.

CHESTERFIELD FC

Founded: 1866	**Record Attendance:** 30,968 (7/4/39)
Turned Professional: 1891	**Colours:** Shirts — Blue with White pin-
Limited Company: 1921	stripes Shorts — White
Admitted to League: 1899	**Telephone No.:** (0246) 209765
Former Name(s): Chesterfield Town FC	**Ticket Information:** (0246) 209765
Nickname: 'Spireites', 'Blues'	**Pitch Size:** 112 x 73yds
Ground: Recreation Ground, Saltgergate,	**Ground Capacity:** 11,308
Chesterfield S40 4SX	**Seating Capacity:** 2,608

GENERAL INFORMATION
Supporters Club Administrator: Roy Frisby
Address: 76 Park Road, Chesterfield
Telephone Number: (0246) 39814
Car Parking: Saltergate Car Parks (½ mile)
Coach Parking: By Police Direction
Nearest Railway Station: Chesterfield (1 mile)
Nearest Bus Station: Chesterfield
Club Shop:
Opening Times: Matchdays only
Telephone No.: (0246) 209765
Postal Sales: Yes
Nearest Police Station: Chesterfield (¾ mile)
Police Force: Derbyshire
Police Telephone Number: (0246) 220100

GROUND INFORMATION
Away Supporters' Entrances: Cross Street Turnstiles
Away Supporters' Sections: Cross Street End (Open)
Family Facilities: Location of Stand: Main Stand — Saltergate Corner
Capacity of Stand: 400
Away Families: None

DISABLED SUPPORTERS INFORMATION
Wheelchairs: Accommodated (Limited Number)
Disabled Toilets: Yes
The Blind: No special facilities

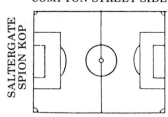

COMPTON STREET SIDE

SALTERGATE SPION KOP

CROSS STREET END (Away)

MAIN STAND
ST. MARGARET'S DRIVE

Travelling Supporters Information:
Routes: From North: Exit M1 Junction 30 then take A619 into Town Centre. Follow signs Old Brampton into Saltergate; From South & East: Take A617 into Town Centre (then as North); From West: Take A619 1st exit at Roundabout, when into Town into Foljambe Road and follow to end, turn right into Saltergate.

COVENTRY CITY FC

Founded: 1883	**Record Attendance:** 51,455 (29/4/67)
Turned Professional: 1893	**Colours:** Shirts — Sky Blue/Navy & White
Limited Company: 1907	Stripes Shorts — Navy with Sky Blue &
Admitted to League: 1919	White Quarters
Former Name(s): Singers FC (1883-1898)	**Telephone No.:** (0203) 257171
Nickname: 'Sky Blues'	**Ticket Information:** (0203) 258879
Ground: Highfield Road Stadium,	**Pitch Size:** 110 x 76yds
King Richard Street, Coventry	**Ground Capacity:** 25,550
CV2 4FW	**Seating Capacity:** 17,650

GENERAL INFORMATION
Supporters Club Administrator: The Secretary
Address: — Coventry City Supporters Club, Freehold Street, Coventry
Telephone Number: —
Car Parking: Street Parking
Coach Parking: Gosford Green Car Park (Adjacent)
Nearest Railway Station: Coventry (1 mile)
Nearest Bus Station: Coventry (1 mile)
Club Shop:
Opening Times: Daily except Sunday (Office hours)
Telephone No.: (0203) 257171
Postal Sales: Yes
Nearest Police Station: Little Park Street, Coventry (1 mile)
Police Force: West Midlands
Police Telephone Number: (0203) 555333

GROUND INFORMATION
Away Supporters' Entrances: Thackhall Street (Tickets from Away club)
Away Supporters' Sections: Sky Blue Stand & East Terrace
Family Facilities: Location of Stand: No special area
Capacity of Stand: —

DISABLED SUPPORTERS INFORMATION
Wheelchairs: Accommodated in Disabled Section (away fans book in advance)
Disabled Toilets: Yes
The Blind: No special facilities

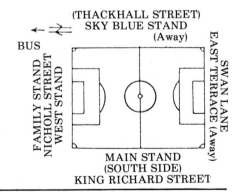

Travelling Supporters Information:
Routes: From North West & South: Exit M6 junction 2. Take A4600 and follow signs for 'City Centre'. Follow this road for approximately 3 miles and, just under railway bridge turn right at traffic lights into Swan Lane. Stadium on left. From East: Take M45 then A45 to Ryton-on-Dunsmore. Take 3rd exit at roundabout (1½ mls) A423, after 1¼ ml. turn right (B4110), follow to T-junction, left then right into Swan Lane.
Bus Services: Service 25 from Railway Station to Bus Station. Services 16, 17, 32 & 33 from Bus Station.

CREWE ALEXANDRA FC

Founded: 1877	**Record Attendance:** 20,000 (30/1/60)
Turned Professional: 1893	**Colours:** Shirts — Red
Limited Company: 1892	Shorts — White
Admitted to League: 1892	**Telephone No.:** (0270) 213014
Former Name(s): None	**Ticket Information:** (0270) 213014
Nickname: 'Railwaymen'	**Pitch Size:** 112 x 74yds
Ground: Gresty Road Ground, Crewe,	**Ground Capacity:** 7,200
Cheshire CW2 6EB	**Seating Capacity:** 1,200

GENERAL INFORMATION
Supporters Club Administrator: Glynn Steele
Address: 18 Gresty Road, Crewe
Telephone Number: (0270) 255206
Car Parking: Car Park at Ground (200 cars)
Coach Parking: Car Park at Ground
Nearest Railway Station: Crewe (5 minutes walk)
Nearest Bus Station: Crewe Town
Club Shop:
Opening Times: Monday-Friday 9.00-5.00 & Matchdays
Telephone No.: (0270) 213014
Postal Sales: Yes
Nearest Police Station: Crewe Town (1 mile)
Police Force: Cheshire
Police Telephone Number: (0270) 500222

GROUND INFORMATION
Away Supporters' Entrances: Gresty Road entrances
Away Supporters' Sections: Gresty Road End
Family Facilities: Location of Stand: Family Stand
Capacity of Stand: 200
Away Families: Yes

DISABLED SUPPORTERS INFORMATION
Wheelchairs: Accommodated (Limited Number)
Disabled Toilets: None
The Blind: Commentaries Available

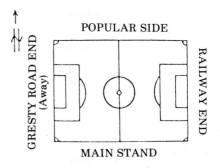

Travelling Supporters Information:
Routes: From North: Exit M6 junction 17 take Crewe (A534) Road, and at Crewe roundabout follow Chester signs into Nantwich Road. Take next left into Gresty Road; From South & East: Take A52 to A5020 to Crewe roundabout (then as North); From West: Take A534 into Crewe and turn right just before railway station into Gresty Road

CRYSTAL PALACE FC

Founded: 1905 **Turned Professional:** 1905 **Limited Company:** 1905 **Admitted to League:** 1920 **Former Name(s):** None **Nickname:** 'Eagles' **Ground:** Selhurst Park, London **SE25 6PU**	**Record Attendance:** 51,482 (11/5/79) **Colours:** Shirts — Red with Blue Stripes Shorts — Red **Telephone No.:** (081) 653 4462 **Ticket Information:** (081) 653 4462 **Pitch Size:** 110 x 75yds **Ground Capacity:** 29,949 **Seating Capacity:** 15,135

GENERAL INFORMATION
Supporters Club Administrator: Terry Byfield
Address: c/o Club
Telephone Number: (081) 653 4462
Car Parking: Street Parking
Coach Parking: Thornton Heath
Nearest Railway Station: Selhurst /Norwood Junction/Thornton Heath
Nearest Bus Station: Norwood Junction
Club Shop:
Opening Times: Weekdays & Matchdays 9.30-5.30
Telephone No.: (081) 653 5584
Postal Sales: Yes
Nearest Police Station: South Norwood (15 minutes walk)
Police Force: Metropolitan
Police Telephone Number: (081) 653 8568

GROUND INFORMATION
Away Supporters' Entrances: Park Road/ Holmesdale Road
Away Supporters' Sections: Corner — Park Road & Holmesdale Road (Open Terrace & Covered Seating)
Family Facilities: Location of Stand: Members Stand (Clifton Road End)
Capacity of Stand: 4,600

DISABLED SUPPORTERS INFORMATION
Wheelchairs: Accommodated, Disabled Section in Arthur Wait Stand. (Park Road Entrance, free of charge)
Disabled Toilets: Yes in Crystals Banquet Suite
The Blind: Commentaries

PARK ROAD
ARTHUR WAIT STAND
ARTHUR WAIT ENCLOSURE

WHITEHORSE LANE
MEMBERS TERRACE

HOLMESDALE ROAD (Away)

MEMBERS STAND
CLIFTON ROAD

Travelling Supporters Information:
Routes: From North: Take M1/A1 to North Circular (A406) to Chiswick. Take South Circular (A205) to Wandsworth, take A3 to A214 and follow signs to Streatham to A23. Turn left onto B273 (1 mile), follow to end and turn left into High Street and into Whitehorse Lane; From East: Take A232 (Croydon Road) to Shirley and join A215 (Norwood Road), after 2¼ miles take left into Whitehorse Lane; From South: Take A23 and follow signs Crystal Palace B266 through Thornton Heath into Whitehorse Lane; From West: Take M4 to Chiswick (then as North).

DARLINGTON FC

Founded: 1883	**Record Attendance:** 21,023 (14/11/60)
Turned Professional: 1908	**Colours:** Shirts — White/Black
Limited Company: 1891	Shorts — Black
Admitted to League: 1921	**Telephone No.:** (0325) 465097
Former Name(s): None	**Ticket Information:** (0325) 467712
Nickname: 'Quakers'	**Pitch Size:** 110 x 74yds
Ground: Feethams Ground, Darlington	**Ground Capacity:** 9,868
DL1 5JB	**Seating Capacity:** 1,120

GENERAL INFORMATION
Supporters Club Administrator:
K. Lett
Address: 60 Harrison Terrace, Darlington
Telephone Number: (0325) 350161
Car Parking: Street Parking
Coach Parking: By Police direction
Nearest Railway Station: Darlington
Nearest Bus Station: Darlington Central
Club Shop:
Opening Times: Monday-Saturday 9.00-5.00
Telephone No.: (0325) 481212
Postal Sales: Yes
Nearest Police Station: Park Police Station, Darlington (¼ mile)
Police Force: Durham
Police Telephone Number: (0325) 467681

GROUND INFORMATION
Away Supporters' Entrances: Polam Lane Turnstiles
Away Supporters' Sections: West Stand (Open and Covered)
Family Facilities: Location of Stand: East Stand
Capacity of Stand: 200
Away Families: None

DISABLED SUPPORTERS INFORMATION
Wheelchairs: Accommodated in Disabled Section in East Stand
Disabled Toilets: None
The Blind: No special facilities

WEST STAND (Away)

POLAM LANE / SOUTH END

FEETHAMS CRICKET GROUND / VICTORIA ROAD

EAST STAND
RIVER SKERNE

Travelling Supporters Information:
Routes: From North: Take A1 (M) to A167 and follow road to Town Centre, then follow Northallerton signs to Victoria Road; From East: Take A67 to Town Centre (then as North); From South: Take A1(M) A66(M) to A66 into Town, 4th exit at roundabout into Victoria Road; From West: Take A67 into Town Centre and 3rd exit at roundabout into Victoria Road.

DERBY COUNTY FC

Founded: 1884	**Record Attendance:** 41,826 (20/9/69)
Turned Professional: 1884	**Colours:** Shirts — White
Limited Company: 1896	Shorts — Black
Admitted to League: 1888 (Founder)	**Telephone No.:** (0332) 40105
Former Name(s): None	**Ticket Information:** (0332) 40105
Nickname: 'Rams'	**Pitch Size:** 110 x 71yds
Ground: Baseball Ground, Shaftesbury	**Ground Capacity:** 23,800
Crescent, Derby DE3 8NB	**Seating Capacity:** 14,500

GENERAL INFORMATION
Supporters Club Administrator: Mr. E. Hallam
Address: c/o Club
Telephone Number: — (0332) 40105
Car Parking: Numerous Car Parks within ½ mile
Coach Parking: Russell St. Derby
Nearest Railway Station: Derby Midland (1 mile) and Ramsline Halt (specials only)
Nearest Bus Station: Derby Central
Club Shop:
Opening Times: Weekdays 9.00-5.00 & Matches
Telephone No.: (0332) 292081
Postal Sales: Yes
Nearest Police Station: Cotton Lane, Derby
Police Force: Derbyshire
Police Telephone Number: (0332) 290100

GROUND INFORMATION
Away Supporters' Entrances: Osmaston Terrace — Turnstiles 51-55
Away Supporters' Sections: Osmaston Middle & Lower Tier (seats)
Family Facilities: Location of Stand: Vulcan Street End
Capacity of Stand: 3,500

DISABLED SUPPORTERS INFORMATION
Wheelchairs: Accommodated in Disabled Section (Normanton End)
Disabled Toilets: Yes
The Blind: Special Facilities Provided

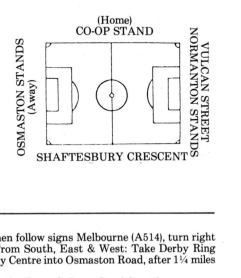

Travelling Supporters Information:
Routes: From North: Take A38 into City Centre then follow signs Melbourne (A514), turn right before Railway Bridge into Shaftesbury Street. From South, East & West: Take Derby Ring Road to Junction with A514 and follow signs to City Centre into Osmaston Road, after 1¼ miles take left turn into Shaftesbury Street.
Bus Services: Services 159, 188 and 189 pass near the Ground. Some Special services.

DONCASTER ROVERS FC

Founded: 1879	**Record Attendance:** 37,149 (2/10/48)
Turned Professional: 1885	**Colours:** Shirts — White with Red trim
Limited Company: 1920	Shorts — White
Admitted to League: 1901	**Telephone No.:** (0302) 539441
Former Name(s): None	**Ticket Information:** (0302) 539441
Nickname: 'Rovers'	**Pitch Size:** 110 x 76yds
Ground: Belle Vue, Bawtry Road,	**Ground Capacity:** 6,535
Doncaster DN4 5HT	**Seating Capacity:** 1,259

GENERAL INFORMATION
Supporters Club Administrator: K. Avis
Address: 64 Harrowden Road, Wheatley, Doncaster
Telephone Number: (0302) 365440
Car Parking: Large Car Park at Ground
Coach Parking: Car Park at Ground
Nearest Railway Station: Doncaster (1½ miles)
Nearest Bus Station: Doncaster
Club Shop:
Opening Times: Tuesdays, Fridays & match days 10.00 a.m.-4 p.m.
Telephone No.: (0302) 539441
Postal Sales: Yes
Nearest Police Station: College Road, Doncaster
Police Force: South Yorkshire
Police Telephone Number: (0302) 366744

GROUND INFORMATION
Away Supporters' Entrances: Turnstiles A & 1,2,3,4, 'A' Block
Away Supporters' Sections: Rossington Road (Open) & Main Stand, 'A' Block
Family Facilities: Location of Stand: Main Stand
Capacity of Stand: —

DISABLED SUPPORTERS INFORMATION
Wheelchairs: Accommodated in Disabled Section — 'A' Block
Disabled Toilets: None
The Blind: No Special Facilities

POPULAR SIDE STAND

ROSSINGTON END (Away)

Enclosure
MAIN STAND
BAWTRY ROAD

BUS

Travelling Supporters Information:
Routes: From North: Take A1 to A638 into Town Centre, follow signs to Bawtry (A638), after 1¼ miles take 3rd exit from roundabout into Bawtry Road; From East: Take M18 to A630, after 2¾ miles take 1st exit at roundabout into A18, after 2½ miles take 1st exit at roundabout into Bawtry Road; From South: Take M1 then M18, to A6182. After 2 miles 3rd exit at roundabout S/P 'Scunthorpe A18'. Then after 1¼ miles 3rd exit roundabout into Bawtry Road. From West: Take A635 into Town Centre and follow signs 'Bawtry' (then as South).

EVERTON FC

Founded: 1878	**Record Attendance:** 78,299 (18/9/48)
Turned Professional: 1885	**Colours:** Shirts — Blue
Limited Company: 1892	Shorts — White
Admitted to League: 1888 (Founder)	**Telephone No.:** (051) 521 2020
Former Name(s): St. Domingo's FC 1878/9	**Dial-a-Seat:** (051) 525 1231
Nickname: 'Blues' 'Toffeemen'	**Pitch Size:** 112 x 78yds
Ground: Goodison Park, Goodison Road,	**Ground Capacity:** 38,500
Liverpool L4 4EL	**Seating Capacity:** 31,000

GENERAL INFORMATION
Supporters Club Administrator: The Secretary
Address: 38 City Road, Liverpool 4
Telephone Number: (051) 525 2207 (after 6 p.m.)
Car Parking: Corner of Priory and Utting Avenue
Coach Parking: Priory Road
Nearest Railway Station: Liverpool Lime Street
Nearest Bus Station: Skelhorne Street, Liverpool
Club Shop:
Opening Times: Weekdays and matchdays 9.00-5.00 and Evening matches
Telephone No.: (051) 521 2020
Postal Sales: Yes — Mail Order and Credit Card
Nearest Police Station: Walton Lane, Liverpool
Police Force: Merseyside
Police Telephone Number: (051) 7096010

GROUND INFORMATION
Away Supporters' Entrances: Park End, Goodison Avenue turnstiles
Away Supporters' Sections: Park End terracing and stands
Family Facilities: Location of Stand: In front of main stand
Capacity of Stand: 2,080
Away Families: None

DISABLED SUPPORTERS INFORMATION
Wheelchairs: Home supporters with season tickets accommodated
Disabled Toilets: In Disabled Area (Bullens Road) 20 wheelchairs and attendants
The Blind: Commentaries Available

BULLENS ROAD

GWLADYS STREET STAND

PARK END TERRACING
GOODISON AVENUE (Away)

GOODISON ROAD
MAIN STAND

↓ BUS

Travelling Supporters Information:
Routes: From North: Exit M6 junction 28. Take A58 Liverpool Road to A580 and follow into Walton Hall Avenue. From South and East: Exit M6 junction 21A to M62. At end of M62 turn right into Queen's Drive. After 3¾ miles turn left into Walton Hall Avenue. From North Wales: Cross Mersey into City Centre and follow signs to Preston (A580) into Walton Hall Avenue.
Bus Services: Service from City Centre — 30, 92, 92A/B, 93.

EXETER CITY FC

Founded: 1904	**Record Attendance:** 20,984 (4/3/31)
Turned Professional: 1908	**Colours:** Shirts — Red & White Stripes
Limited Company: 1908	Shorts — Black
Admitted to League: 1920	**Telephone No.:** (0392) 54073
Former Name(s): Formed by amalgamation of St. Sidwell Utd FC & Exeter Utd	**Ticket Information:** (0392) 54073
Nickname: 'Grecians'	**Pitch Size:** 114 x 73yds
Ground: St. James Park, Exeter EX4 6PX	(FC **Ground Capacity:** 8,898
	Seating Capacity: 1,608

GENERAL INFORMATION
Supporters Club Administrator: Mr. K.G. Baker
Address: c/o Club
Telephone Number: (0392) 59466
Car Parking: Limited Street Parking
Coach Parking: Paris Street Bus Station
Nearest Railway Station: Exeter St. James Park (adjacent)
Nearest Bus Station: Paris Street Bus Station
Club Shop:
Opening Times: Weekdays & Matchdays 9.00-4.00
Telephone No.: (0392) 54073
Postal Sales: Yes
Nearest Police Station: Heavitree Rd., Exeter (½ ml)
Police Force: Devon & Cornwall
Police Telephone Number: (0392) 52101

GROUND INFORMATION
Away Supporters' Entrances: St. James Road Turnstiles
Away Supporters' Sections: St. James Road Enclosure
Family Facilities: Location of Stand: Block C Grandstand
Capacity of Stand: —

DISABLED SUPPORTERS INFORMATION
Wheelchairs: Limited accommodation at front of stand
Disabled Toilets: None
The Blind: No Special Facilities

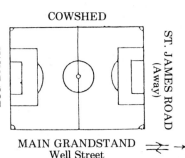

Travelling Supporters Information:
Routes: From North: Exit M5 junction 30 and follow signs to City Centre along Sidmouth Road to Heavitree Road take 4th exit at roundabout into Western Way and 2nd exit Tiverton Road, next left into St. James Road. From East: Take A30 into Heavitree Road (then as North); From South & West: Take A38 and follow City Centre signs into Western Way and 3rd exit at roundabout into St. James Road.
Bus Services: Services A,D,J,K & S from City Centre

FULHAM FC

Founded: 1879	**Record Attendance:** 49,335 (8/10/38)
Turned Professional: 1898	**Colours:** Shirts — White
Limited Company: 1903	Shorts — Black
Admitted to League: 1907	**Telephone No.:** (071) 736 6561
Former Name(s): Fulham St. Andrew's FC	**Ticket Information:** (071) 736 6561
(1879-1898)	**Pitch Size:** 110 x 75yds
Nickname: 'Cottagers'	**Ground Capacity:** 17,934
Ground: Craven Cottage, Stevenage Road,	**Seating Capacity:** 6,610
Fulham, London SW6 6HH	

GENERAL INFORMATION
Supporters Club Administrator: The Chairman
Address: c/o The Club
Telephone Number: (071) 736 6561
Car Parking: Street Parking
Coach Parking: Stevenage Road
Nearest Railway Station: Putney
Nearest Tube Station: Putney Bridge (District)
Club Shop:
Opening Times: Home Matchdays and by prior arrangement (phone)
Telephone No.: (071) 736 6561
Postal Sales: Yes
Nearest Police Station: Heckfield Place, Fulham
Police Force: Metropolitan
Police Telephone Number: (071) 741 6212

GROUND INFORMATION
Away Supporters' Entrances: Putney End
Away Supporters' Sections: Putney Terrace (Open)
Family Facilities: Location of Stand: Miller Stand ('S' Block)
Capacity of Stand: 350
Away Families: Accommodated in Disabled Section

DISABLED SUPPORTERS INFORMATION
Wheelchairs: Accommodated in Disabled Section — alongside Miller Stand touchline
Disabled Toilets: None
The Blind: Commentaries by prior arrangement

STEVENAGE ROAD
MAIN STAND (COTTAGE)

HAMMERSMITH END

PUTNEY END (Away)

ERIC MILLER STAND
River Thames

Travelling Supporters Information:
Routes: From North: Take A1/M1 to North Circular (A406) West to Neasden and follow signs Harlesdon A404, then Hammersmith A219. At Broadway follow Fulham sign and turn right (1 mile) into Harbord Street left at end to Ground; From South & East: Take South Circular (A205) and follow Putney Bridge sign (A219), Cross Bridge and follow Hammersmith signs for ½ mile, left into Bishops Park Road, then right at end; From West: Take M4 to A4 then branch left (2 miles) into Hammersmith Broadway (then as North).
Bus Services: Services 30, 74, 85, 95 & 220 from tube station to Ground.

GILLINGHAM FC

Founded: 1893	**Record Attendance:** 23,002 (10/1/48)
Turned Professional: 1894	**Colours:** Shirts — Blue
Limited Company: 1893	Shorts — White
Admitted to League: 1920	**Telephone No.:** (0634) 51854/51462
Former Name(s): New Brompton FC	**Ticket Information:** (0634) 576828
(1893/1913)	**Pitch Size:** 114 x 75yds
Nickname: 'Gills'	**Ground Capacity:** 10,412
Ground: Priestfield Stadium, Redfern	**Seating Capacity:** 1,092
Avenue, Gillingham, Kent ME7 4DD	

GENERAL INFORMATION
Supporters Club Administrator: The Chairman
Address: c/o Club
Telephone Number: (0634) 51854
Car Parking: Street Parking
Coach Parking: By Police direction
Nearest Railway Station: Gillingham
Nearest Bus Station: Gillingham
Club Shop: Redfern Avenue
Opening Times: Weekdays and matchdays 10.00-3.00
Telephone No.: (0634) 51462
Postal Sales: Yes
Nearest Police Station: Gillingham
Police Force: Kent
Police Telephone Number: (0634) 34488

GROUND INFORMATION
Away Supporters' Entrances: Redfern Avenue turnstiles
Away Supporters' Sections: Redfern Avenue corner (Gillingham end)
Family Facilities: Location of Stand: Main Stand (Rainham End)
Capacity of Stand: 1,090
Away Families: None

DISABLED SUPPORTERS INFORMATION
Wheelchairs: Accommodated in disabled section adjacent to Main Stand (use Redfern Avenue entrance) — prior application preferred
Disabled Toilets: None
The Blind: No Special Facilities

GORDON ROAD STAND

TORONTO ROAD RAINHAM END

GILLINGHAM END Priestfield Road

MAIN STAND
Redfern Avenue

Travelling Supporters Information:
Routes: From All Parts: Exit M2 junction 4 and follow link road (dual carriageway) B278 to 3rd roundabout. Turn left on to A2 (dual carriageway) across roundabout to traffic lights. Turn right Woodlands Road — after traffic lights. Ground ¼ mile on left.

GRIMSBY TOWN FC

Founded: 1878	**Record Attendance:** 31,651 (20/2/37)
Turned Professional: 1890	**Colours:** Shirts — Black & White stripes
Limited Company: 1890	Shorts — Black
Admitted to League: 1892	**Telephone No.:** (0472) 697111
Former Name(s): Grimsby Pelham FC	**Ticket Information:** (0472) 697111
(1879- 9)	**Pitch Size:** 111 x 74yds
Nickname: 'Mariners'	**Ground Capacity:** 17,526
Ground: Blundell Park, Cleethorpes	**Seating Capacity:** 5,021
DN35 7PY	

GENERAL INFORMATION
Supporters Club Administrator: Rachel Branson
Address: 26 Humberstone Road, Grimsby
Telephone Number: (0472) 360050
Car Parking: Street Parking
Coach Parking: Harrington Street — near Ground
Nearest Railway Station: Cleethorpes (1½ miles), New Clee (½ mile — for Specials Only)
Nearest Bus Station: Brighowgate, Grimsby (4 miles)
Club Shop:
Opening Times: Monday-Friday 10.00-4.00. Match Saturdays 10.00-Kick-off
Telephone No.: (0472) 699889
Postal Sales: Yes
Nearest Police Station: Cleethorpes (Near Railway Station) 1½ miles
Police Force: Humberside
Police Telephone Number: (0472) 697131

GROUND INFORMATION
Away Supporters' Entrances: Harrington Street Turnstiles 15-20 (Near Blundell Avenue)
Away Supporters' Sections: Osmond Stand Covered standing and seats
Family Facilities: Location of Stand: Main Stand (with access to family lounge)
Capacity of Stand: 120

DISABLED SUPPORTERS INFORMATION
Wheelchairs: Accommodated in Disabled Section — Main Stand
Disabled Toilets: Yes
The Blind: Commentaries in Disabled Section

(CLEETHORPES) Grimsby Road To Grimsby

FINDUS STAND

Neville Street
OSMOND STAND (Away)

Blundell Avenue
PONTOON STAND

MAIN STAND
Harrington Street

Travelling Supporters Information:
Routes: From All Parts except Lincolnshire and East Anglia: Take M180 to A180 follow signs to Grimsby/Cleethorpes. A180 ends at roundabout (3rd in short distance after crossing Docks), take 2nd exit from roundabout over railway flyover into Cleethorpes Road (A1098) and continue into Cleethorpes Road (A1098), continue into Grimsby Road. After second stretch of Dual Carriageway Ground ½ mile on left; From Lincolnshire: Take A46 or A16 and follow Cleethorpes signs along (A1098) Weelsby Road (2 miles) and take 1st exit at roundabout at end of Clee Road into Grimsby Road. Ground 1¾ miles on right.

HALIFAX TOWN FC

Founded: 1911	**Record Attendance:** 36,885 (14/2/53)
Turned Professional: 1911	**Colours:** Shirts — Blue & White
Limited Company: 1911	Shorts — White
Admitted to League: 1921	**Telephone No.:** (0422) 353423
Former Name(s): None	**Ticket Information:** (0422) 353423
Nickname: 'Shaymen'	**Pitch Size:** 110 x 70yds
Ground: Shay Ground, Shay Syke,	**Ground Capacity:** 7,503
Halifax, HX1 2YS	**Seating Capacity:** 1,878

GENERAL INFORMATION
Supporters Club Administrator: Paul Kendall
Address: Halifax Town Promotions, Shay Ground, Halifax
Telephone Number: (0422) 361582
Car Parking: Shaw Hill Car Park (nearby)
Coach Parking: Calderdale bus depot (Shaw Hill)
Nearest Railway Station: Halifax (3 minutes walk)
Nearest Bus Station: Halifax
Club Shop:
Opening Times: Weekdays 9.30-5.00 (Except Thursday) and match days
Telephone No.: (0422) 361582
Postal Sales: Yes
Nearest Police Station: Halifax (¼ mile)
Police Force: West Yorkshire
Police Telephone Number: (0422) 360333

GROUND INFORMATION
Away Supporters' Entrances: Shay Syke turnstiles
Away Supporters' Sections: Visitor's enclosure, Shay Syke
Family Facilities: Location of Stand: Family & Disabled Stand
Capacity of Stand: 364 seats, 85 standing
Away Families: Yes

DISABLED SUPPORTERS INFORMATION
Wheelchairs: Accommodated in Disabled Section
Disabled Toilets: Yes
The Blind: No Special Facilities

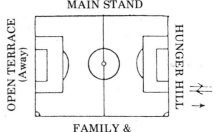

Huddersfield Road (A629)
MAIN STAND
OPEN TERRACE (Away)
HUNGER HILL
FAMILY & DISABLED STAND

Travelling Supporters Information:
Routes: From North: Take A629 to Halifax Town Centre. Take 2nd exit at roundabout into Broad Street and follow signs for Huddersfield (A629) into Skircoat Road. From South, East and West: Exit M62 junction 24 and follow Halifax (A629) signs to town centre into Skircoat Road for ground.

HARTLEPOOL UNITED FC

Founded: 1908	**Record Attendance:** 17,426 (15/1/57)
Turned Professional: 1908	**Colours:** Shirts — Blue
Limited Company: 1908	Shorts — White
Admitted to League: 1921	**Telephone No.:** (0429) 272584
Former Name(s): Hartlepools Utd. FC	**Ticket Information:** (0429) 222077
(1908/68): Hartlepool FC (1968/77)	**Fax:** (0429) 863007
Nickname: 'The Pool'	**Pitch Size:** 113 x 77yds
Ground: Victoria Ground, Clarence Road,	**Ground Capacity:** 9,607
Hartlepool. TS24 8BZ	**Seating Capacity:** 1,500

GENERAL INFORMATION
Supporters Club Administrator: Ian Newton
Address: 49 Middleton Road, Hartlepool
Telephone Number: (0429) 279412
Car Parking: Street Parking & rear of Clock Garage
Coach Parking: United Bus Station
Nearest Railway Station: Hartlepool Church Street (5 minutes walk)
Nearest Bus Station: United Bus Station
Club Shop:
Opening Times: Weekdays 9.00-5.00, Saturdays 9.00-2.30
Telephone No.: (0429) 222077
Postal Sales: Yes
Nearest Police Station: Avenue Road, Hartlepool
Police Force: Cleveland
Police Telephone Number: (0429) 221151

GROUND INFORMATION
Away Supporters' Entrances: Clarence Road Turnstiles 1, 2, & 3.
Away Supporters' Sections: Town End, Clarence Road
Family Facilities: Location of Stand: None
Capacity of Stand: —
Away Families: None

DISABLED SUPPORTERS INFORMATION
Wheelchairs: Accommodated in Disabled Section on Mill House side of ground
Disabled Toilets: None
The Blind: Commentaries available

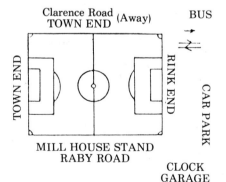

Travelling Supporters Information:
Routes: From North: Take A1/A19 then A179 towards Hartlepool to Hart. Straight across traffic lights (2½ miles) to cross-roads, then turn left into Clarence Road. From South and West: Take A1/A19 or A689 into town centre then bear left into Clarence Road.

HEREFORD UNITED FC

Founded: 1924	**Record Attendance:** 18,114 (4/1/58)
Turned Professional: 1924	**Colours:** Shirts — White
Limited Company: 1939	Shorts — Black
Admitted to League: 1972	**Telephone No.:** (0432) 276666
Former Name(s): None	**Ticket Information:** (0432) 276666
Nickname: 'United'	**Pitch Size:** 111 x 74yds
Ground: Edgar Street, Hereford	**Ground Capacity:** 13,777
HR4 9JU	**Seating Capacity:** 2,897

GENERAL INFORMATION
Supporters Club Administrator: Mr. J. Rogers
Address: c/o Club
Telephone Number: (0432) 265005
Car Parking: Merton Meadow and Edgar Street car parks
Coach Parking: Cattle Market (near ground)
Nearest Railway Station: Hereford (½ mile)
Nearest Bus Station: Commercial Road, Hereford
Club Shop:
Opening Times: Matchdays & Weekdays via Commercial Office
Telephone No.: (0432) 276666
Postal Sales: Yes
Nearest Police Station: Bath Street, Hereford
Police Force: Hereford
Police Telephone Number: (0432) 276422

GROUND INFORMATION
Away Supporters' Entrances: Blackfriars Street and Edgar Street
Away Supporters' Sections: Blackfriars Street end
Family Facilities: Location of Stand: Edgar Street side
Capacity of Stand: 300

DISABLED SUPPORTERS INFORMATION
Wheelchairs: Accommodated in Disabled Section Edgar Street Side
Disabled Toilets: None
The Blind: No Special Facilities

EDGAR STREET

BLACKFRIARS STREET END (Away)

MERTON MEADOW TERRACES

MERTON MEADOW STANDS

Travelling Supporters Information:
Routes: From North: Follow A49 Hereford signs straight into Edgar Street. From East: Take A465 or A438 into Hereford town centre, then follow signs for Leominster (A49) into Edgar Street. From South: Take A49 or A465 into town centre (then as East). From West: Take A438 into town centre (then as East)

HUDDERSFIELD TOWN FC

Founded: 1908
Turned Professional: 1908
Limited Company: 1908
Admitted to League: 1910
Former Name(s): None
Nickname: 'Terriers'
Ground: Leeds Road, Huddersfield
HD1 6PE

Record Attendance: 67,037 (27/2/32)
Colours: Shirts — Blue & White stripes
Shorts — White
Telephone No.: (0484) 420335
Ticket Information: (0484) 420335
Pitch Size: 115 x 75yds
Ground Capacity: 15,520
Seating Capacity: 5,500

GENERAL INFORMATION
Supporters Club Administrator: Mrs A. Sedgwick
Address: c/o Club
Telephone Number: (0484) 420335
Car Parking: Car Park for 1,000 cars adjacent
Coach Parking: Adjacent car park
Nearest Railway Station: Huddersfield (1¼ miles)
Nearest Bus Station: Huddersfield
Club Shop:
Opening Times: Weekdays and match days 9.00-5.00
Telephone No.: (0484) 534867
Postal Sales: Yes
Nearest Police Station: Huddersfield (1 mile)
Police Force: West Yorkshire
Police Telephone Number: (0484) 422122

GROUND INFORMATION
Away Supporters' Entrances: Turnstiles 9-10 (seats); Turnstiles 11-18 (standing)
Away Supporters' Sections: Dalton Bank Terrace (open)
Family Facilities: Location of Stand: Leeds Road End
Capacity of Stand: 1,900
Away Families: None

DISABLED SUPPORTERS INFORMATION
Wheelchairs: Accommodated in Disabled Section in Main Stand
Disabled Toilets: Yes
The Blind: No Special Facilities

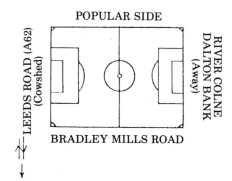

Travelling Supporters Information:
Routes: From North, East & West: Exit M62 junction 25 and take the A644 and A62 following Huddersfield signs. Stadium on left side of A62 (Leeds Road) 1 mile before town centre. From South: Enter Huddersfield on A629. At Ring Road follow signs A62 (Leeds Road) Stadium on right (1 mile)
Bus Services: 220, 221, 201/2/3

HULL CITY FC

Founded: 1904	**Record Attendance:** 55,019 (26/2/49)
Turned Professional: 1904	**Colours:** Shirts — Amber & Black stripes
Limited Company: 1904	Amber sleeves Shorts — Black
Admitted to League: 1905	**Telephone No.:** (0482) 51119
Former Name(s): None	**Ticket Information:** (0482) 51119
Nickname: 'Tigers'	**Pitch Size:** 112 x 72yds
Ground: Boothferry Park, Boothferry	**Ground Capacity:** 17,380
Road, Hull. HU4 6EU	**Seating Capacity:** 5,294

GENERAL INFORMATION
Supporters Club Administrator:
S.C.A. Riby
Address: c/o Club
Telephone Number: (0482) 446878
Car Parking: Limited parking at ground. Street parking
Coach Parking: At ground
Nearest Railway Station: Hull Paragon (1½ miles)
Nearest Bus Station: Ferensway, Hull (1½ miles)
Club Shop:
Opening Times: Weekdays 9.30-4.30. Matchdays 10.00-3.00
Telephone No.: (0482) 51119/28297
Postal Sales: Yes
Nearest Police Station: Priory Road, Hull (2 miles)
Police Force: Humberside
Police Telephone Number: (0482) 512111

GROUND INFORMATION
Away Supporters' Entrances: North Stand turnstiles
Away Supporters' Sections: Visitor's enclosure, North Stand
Family Facilities: Location of Stand: Main Stand
Capacity of Stand: 568

DISABLED SUPPORTERS INFORMATION
Wheelchairs: Accommodated in Disabled Enclosure, South East corner
Disabled Toilets: Yes
The Blind: Commentaries Available

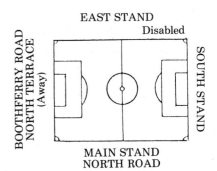

Travelling Supporters Information:
Routes: From North: Take A1 or A19 then A1079 into city centre and follow signs for Leeds (A63) into Anlaby Road. At roundabout (1 mile) take 1st exit into Boothferry Road. From West: Take M62 to A63 to Hull. Fork left after Ferriby Crest Motel to Humber Bridge roundabout, then take 1st exit to Boothferry Road (Ground 1½ miles). Do NOT follow Clive Sullivan way. From South: non-scenic alternative route take M18 to M62 (then as West). Or use motorways M1 to M18 then M180 and follow signs over Humber Bridge (Toll), take 2nd exit at roundabout (A63) towards Boothferry Road (ground 1½ miles).

IPSWICH TOWN FC

Founded: 1887
Turned Professional: 1936
Limited Company: 1936
Admitted to League: 1938
Former Name(s): None
Nickname: 'Town' 'Super Blues'
Ground: Portman Road, Ipswich
IP1 2DA

Record Attendance: 38,010 (8/3/75)
Colours: Shirts — Blue
Shorts — White
Telephone No.: (0473) 219211
Ticket Information: (0473) 219211
Pitch Size: 112 x 70yds
Ground Capacity: 28,645
Seating Capacity: 14,000

GENERAL INFORMATION
Supporters Club Administrator: Mr. G. Dodson
Address: c/o Club
Telephone Number: (0473) 219211
Car Parking: Portman Road and Portman Walk car parks
Coach Parking: Portman Walk
Nearest Railway Station: Ipswich (5 minutes walk)
Nearest Bus Station: Ipswich
Club Shop:
Opening Times: Weekdays & matchdays 9.00-5.00
Telephone No.: (0473) 219211
Postal Sales: Yes
Nearest Police Station: Civic Drive, Ipswich (5 minutes walk)
Police Force: Suffolk
Police Telephone Number: (0473) 55811

GROUND INFORMATION
Away Supporters' Entrances: Portman Walk turnstiles
Away Supporters' Sections: Visitor's section, North Stand (covered)
Family Facilities: Location of Stand: South side Pioneer Stand
Capacity of Stand: 2,200

DISABLED SUPPORTERS INFORMATION
Wheelchairs: Accommodated in disabled section in Churchmans Stand
Disabled Toilets: Yes
The Blind: Commentaries available

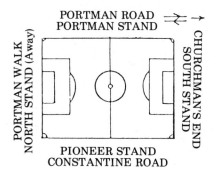

Travelling Supporters Information:
Routes: From North and West: Take A45 following signs for Ipswich West only. Proceed through Post House traffic lights and at 2nd roundabout turn right into West End Road, ground ¼ mile along on left. From South: Follow signs for Ipswich West then as North and West.

LEEDS UNITED FC

Founded: 1919
Turned Professional: 1919
Limited Company: 1919
Admitted to League: 1920
Former Name(s): Formed after Leeds City
FC wound up for 'Irregular Practices'
Nickname: 'United'
Ground: Elland Road, Leeds LS11 OES

Record Attendance: 57,892 (15/3/67)
Colours: Shirts — White
Shorts — White
Telephone No.: (0532) 716037
Ticket Information: (0532) 710710
Pitch Size: 117 x 76yds
Ground Capacity: 32,000
Seating Capacity: 16,500

GENERAL INFORMATION
Supporters Club Administrator: Eric Carlile
Address: c/o Club
Telephone Number: (0532) 716037
Car Parking: Large Car Parks (Adjacent)
Coach Parking: By Police Direction
Nearest Railway Station: Leeds City
Nearest Bus Station: Leeds City Central — Specials from Swinegate
Club Shop:
Opening Times: Weekdays 9.15-5.00, match days 9.15—kick-off
Telephone No.: (0532) 706844
Postal Sales: Yes (send SAE)
Nearest Police Station: Holbeck, Leeds (3 miles)
Police Force: West Yorkshire
Police Telephone Number: (0532) 435353

GROUND INFORMATION
Away Supporters' Entrances: Lowfield Road
Away Supporters' Sections: Lowfield Road — Pen 5 (Open)
Family Facilities: Location of Stand:
South Stand Paddock
Capacity of Stand: 2,500

DISABLED SUPPORTERS INFORMATION
Wheelchairs: Accommodated in Disabled Section (West Stand)
Disabled Toilets: Yes
The Blind: Commentaries via headphones (West Stand)

LOWFIELD ROAD STAND
(Away)

GELDARD ROAD NORTH STAND

ELLAND ROAD SOUTH STAND

WEST STAND

Travelling Supporters Information:
Routes: From North: Take A58 or A61 into City Centre and follow signs to M621; leave Motorway after 1½ miles and exit roundabout on to A643 into Elland Road; From North East: Take A63 or A64 into City Centre (then as North); From South: Take M1 to M621 (then as North); From West: Take M62 to M621 (then as North).

LEICESTER CITY FC

Founded: 1884	**Record Attendance:** 47,298 (18/2/28)
Turned Professional: 1894	**Colours:** Shirts — Blue with White Collars
Limited Company: 1894	Shorts — White
Admitted to League: 1894	**Telephone No.:** (0533) 555000
Former Name(s): Leicester Fosse FC	**Pitch Size:** 112 x 75yds
(1884-1919)	**Ground Capacity:** 27,600
Nickname: 'Filberts' 'Foxes'	**Seating Capacity:** 15,000
Ground: City Stadium, Filbert Street, Leicester LE2 7FL	

GENERAL INFORMATION
Supporters Club Administrator: C. Ginetta
Address: c/o Club
Telephone Number: (0533) 555000
Car Parking: NCP Car Parks (5 minutes walk) & Street Parking
Coach Parking: Western Boulevard
Nearest Railway Station: Leicester (1 mile)
Nearest Bus Station: St. Margaret's (1 mile)
Club Shop:
Opening Times: Weekdays 9.00-5.00 (closes for lunch), matchdays 10.00-3.00
Telephone No.: (0533) 555000
Postal Sales: Yes
Nearest Police Station: Charles Street, Leicester
Police Force: Leicester
Police Telephone Number: (0533) 530066

GROUND INFORMATION
Away Supporters' Entrances: East Stand, Block T Turnstiles
Away Supporters' Sections: Spion Kop enclosure (covered)/Block T East Stand
Family Facilities: Location of Stand: By Member's Stand
Capacity of Stand: 3,600

DISABLED SUPPORTERS INFORMATION
Wheelchairs: Accommodated. Limited (prior arrangement required)
Disabled Toilets: Available in 1993 season
The Blind: No Special Facilities

MEMBER'S STAND

BLACK PAD
SPION KOP
SOUTH STAND
(Away)

FAMILY CLUB
FILBERT STREET
NORTH STAND

BLOCK
T.
EAST STAND
BURNMOOR STREET

Travelling Supporters Information:
Routes: From North: Take A46/A607 into City Centre or exit M1 Junction 22 for City Centre, follow 'Rugby' signs into Almond Road, turn right at end into Aylestone Road, turn left into Walnut Street and left again into Filbert Street; From East: Take A47 into City Centre (then as for North); From South: Exit M1 Junction 21 and take A46, turn right ¾ mile after railway bridge into Upperton Road, then right into Filbert Street. From West: Take M69 to City Centre (then as North).

LEYTON ORIENT FC

Founded: 1881	**Record Attendance:** 34,345 (25/1/64)
Turned Professional: 1903	**Colours:** Shirts — Red
Limited Company: 1906	Shorts — White
Admitted to League: 1905	**Telephone No.:** (081) 539 2224
Former Name(s): Glyn Cricket & Football	**Ticket Information:** (081) 539 2223
Club (1881/6); Eagle FC (1886/8) Clapton	**Pitch Size:** 115 x 80yds
Orient FC (1888/1946); Leyton Orient FC	**Ground Capacity:** 18,869
(1946/66); Orient FC (1966/87)	**Seating Capacity:** 7,171
Nickname: 'O's'	

Ground: Leyton Stadium, Brisbane Road, Leyton, London E10 5NE

GENERAL INFORMATION
Supporters Club Administrator: D. Dodd
Address: c/o Club
Telephone Number: (081) 539 6156
Car Parking: NCP Brisbane Road & Street Parking
Coach Parking: By Police Direction
Nearest Railway Station: Leyton Midland Road (½ mile)
Nearest Tube Station: Leyton (Central)
Club Shop:
Opening Times: Matchdays only
Telephone No.: (081) 539 2223
Postal Sales: Yes
Nearest Police Station: Francis Road, Leyton, London E10
Police Force: Metropolitan
Police Telephone Number: (081) 556 8855

GROUND INFORMATION
Away Supporters' Entrances: South Terrace Turnstiles
Away Supporters' Sections: South Terrace (Open)
Family Facilities: Location of Stand: North Wing
Capacity of Stand: not specified

DISABLED SUPPORTERS INFORMATION
Wheelchairs: Accommodated in Disabled Section North Terrace
Disabled Toilets: Yes
The Blind: No Special Facilities

```
          OLIVER ROAD
          WEST STAND

BUCKINGHAM ROAD                    WINDSOR ROAD
SOUTH TERRACE (Away)               NORTH TERRACE

          MAIN STAND
          BRISBANE ROAD
```

Travelling Supporters Information:
Routes: From North & West: Take A406 North Circular and follow signs Chelmsford, to Edmonton, after 2½ miles 3rd exit at roundabout towards Leyton (A112). Pass railway station and turn right (½ mile) into Windsor Road and left into Brisbane Road; From East: Follow A12 to London then City for Leytonstone follow Hackney signs into Grove Road, cross Main Road into Ruckholt Road and turn right into Leyton High Road, turn left (¼ mile) into Buckingham Road, then left into Brisbane Road; From South: Take A102M through Blackwall Tunnel and follow signs to Newmarket (A102) to join A11 to Stratford, then signs Stratford Station into Leyton Road to railway station (then as North).

LINCOLN CITY FC

Founded: 1883
Turned Professional: 1892
Limited Company: 1892
Admitted to League: 1892
Former Name(s): None
Nickname: 'Red Imps'
Ground: Sincil Bank, Lincoln
LN5 8LD

Record Attendance: 23,196 (15/11/67)
Colours: Shirts — Red & White stripes
Shorts — Black
Telephone No.: (0522) 522224/510263
Ticket Information: (0522) 522224/510263
Pitch Size: 110 x 75yds
Ground Capacity: 11,500
Seating Capacity: 2,050

GENERAL INFORMATION
Supporters Club Administrator: —
Address: c/o Club
Telephone Number: (0522) 522224/510263
Car Parking: Adjacent
Coach Parking: South Common (300 yards)
Nearest Railway Station: Lincoln Central
Nearest Bus Station: Lincoln Central
Club Shop:
Opening Times: Weekdays & matchdays 9.00-5.00
Telephone No.: (0522) 522224/510263
Postal Sales: Yes
Nearest Police Station: West Parade, Lincoln (1½ miles)
Police Force: Lincolnshire
Police Telephone Number: (0522) 529911

GROUND INFORMATION
Away Supporters' Entrances: South-West Corner, Sincil Bank
Away Supporters' Sections: South-West Corner, Sincil Bank (open) and South Park Stand (covered)
Family Facilities: Location of Stand: Family Stand
Capacity of Stand: 1,450

DISABLED SUPPORTERS INFORMATION
Wheelchairs: Accommodated. Via Turnstiles 1 & 2
Disabled Toilets: Yes
The Blind: No Special Facilities

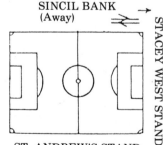

SINCIL BANK (Away)

STACEY WEST STAND

ST. ANDREW'S STAND

Travelling Supporters Information:
Routes: From East: Take A46 or A158 into City Centre following Newark (A46) signs into High Street. Pass under railway bridge and take next left (Queen Street) for Ground; From North & West: Take A15 or A57 into City Centre then as East; From South: Take A1 to A46 for City Centre then into High Street and turn right before railway bridge into Queen Street for Ground.

LIVERPOOL FC

Founded: 1892
Turned Professional: 1892
Limited Company: 1892
Admitted to League: 1893
Former Name(s): None
Nickname: 'Reds'
Ground: Anfield Road, Liverpool
L4 0TH

Record Attendance: 61,905 (2/2/52)
Colours: Shirts — Red with White markings   Shorts — Red with White markings
Telephone No.: (051) 263 2361
Dial-a-Seat: (051) 260 8680
Pitch Size: 110 x 75yds
Ground Capacity: 39,770
Seating Capacity: 23,290

GENERAL INFORMATION
Supporters Club Administrator: Mr. R. Gill
Address: Liverpool Supporters Club, Lower Breck Road, Anfield, Liverpool
Telephone Number: (051) 263 6386
Car Parking: Stanley Park Car Park (adjacent)
Coach Parking: Priory Road & Pinehurst Avenue
Nearest Railway Station: Kirkdale
Nearest Bus Station: Skelhorne Street, Liverpool
Club Shop:
Opening Times: Monday-Saturday 9.30-5.30
Telephone No.: (051) 263 1760
Postal Sales: Yes
Nearest Police Station: Walton Lane, Liverpool (1½ miles)
Police Force: Merseyside
Police Telephone Number: (051) 709 6010

GROUND INFORMATION
Away Supporters' Entrances: Anfield Road
Away Supporters' Sections: Visitors Section, Anfield Road (Covered)
Family Facilities: Location of Stand: Anfield Road End
Capacity of Stand: 1,300
Away Families: None

DISABLED SUPPORTERS INFORMATION
Wheelchairs: Accommodated in Disabled Section (Paddock Enclosure)
Disabled Toilets: Yes
The Blind: Commentaries in Disabled Section

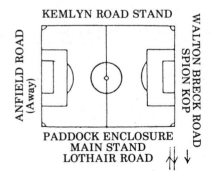

Travelling Supporters Information:
Routes: From North: Exit M6 junction 28 and follow Liverpool A58 signs into Walton Hall Avenue, pass Stanley Park and turn left into Anfield Road; From South and East: Take M62 to end of motorway then turn right into Queen's Drive (A5058) and turn left (3 miles) into Utting Avenue, after 1 mile turn right into Anfield Road; From North Wales: Take Mersey Tunnel into City Centre and follow signs to Preston (A580) into Walton Hall Avenue, turn right into Anfield Road before Stanley Park.

LUTON TOWN FC

Founded: 1885	**Record Attendance:** 30,069 (4/3/59)
Turned Professional: 1890	**Colours:** Shirts — White/Royal Blue/
Limited Company: 1897	Orange Shorts — Blue/Orange/White
Admitted to League: 1897	**Telephone No.:** (0582) 411622
Former Name(s): Formed by amalgama-	**Ticket Information:** (0582) 30748
tion of Wanderers FC & Excelsior FC	**Pitch Size:** 110 x 72yds
Nickname: 'Hatters'	**Ground Capacity:** 13,466
Ground: Kenilworth Road Stadium, 1	**Seating Capacity:** 9,116
Maple Road, Luton LU4 8AW	

GENERAL INFORMATION
Supporters Club Administrator: Mrs P. Gray
Address: 19 Kingsdown Avenue, Luton, Beds.
Telephone Number: (0582) 391574
Car Parking: Street Parking
Coach Parking: Luton Bus Station
Nearest Railway Station: Luton (1 mile)
Nearest Bus Station: Bute Street, Luton
Club Shop: Oak Road
Opening Times: 9.00-5.00
Telephone No.: (0582) 411622
Postal Sales: Yes
Nearest Police Station: Buxton Road, Luton (¾ mile)
Police Force: Bedfordshire
Police Telephone Number: (0582) 401212

GROUND INFORMATION
Away Supporters' Entrances: Oak Road
Away Supporters' Sections: Oak Stand
Family Facilities: Location of Stand: Kenilworth Stand
Capacity of Stand: 5,802
Away Families: Oak Road Stand

DISABLED SUPPORTERS INFORMATION
Wheelchairs: 15 places in Main Stand (book in advance)
Disabled Toilets: Yes
The Blind: Commentaries Available

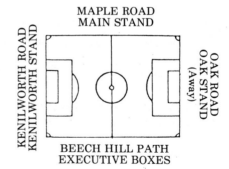

Travelling Supporters Information:
Routes: From North and West: Exit M1 junction 11 and follow signs to Luton (A505) into Dunstable Road. Follow one-way system and turn right back towards Dunstable, take first left into Oak Road. From South and East: Exit M1 junction 10 (or A6/A612) into Luton town centre and follow signs into Dunstable Road. After railway bridge take sixth turning on left into Oak Road.

MAIDSTONE UNITED FC

Founded: 1897	**Record Attendance:** Not applicable
Turned Professional:	**Colours:** Shirts — Amber
Limited Company:	Shorts — Black
Admitted to League: 1989	**Telephone No.:** (0622) 754403
Former Name(s): None	**Ticket Information:** (0622) 756700
Nickname: The Stones	**Pitch Size:** 110 x 75yds
Ground: Watling Street, Stone, Dartford,	**Ground Capacity:** 5,250
Kent	**Seating Capacity:** 720

GENERAL INFORMATION
Supporters Club Administrator: None
Address: —
Telephone Number: —
Car Parking: Street Parking only
Coach Parking: Adjacent to Ground
Nearest Railway Station: Dartford
(1½ miles)
Nearest Bus Station: Dartford
Club Shop:
Opening Times: Matchdays only
Telephone No.: (0622) 754403
Postal Sales: Yes
Nearest Police Station: Dartford (1½ miles)
Police Force: Kent
Police Telephone Number:

GROUND INFORMATION
Away Supporters' Entrances: St. John's Road Turnstiles
Away Supporters' Sections: St. John's Road Side
Family Facilities: Location of Stand:
Family Terrace in front of Main Stand
Capacity of Stand: 720

DISABLED SUPPORTERS INFORMATION
Wheelchairs: Accommodated — Side of Main Stand
Disabled Toilets: Main Stand
The Blind: No Special Facilities

ST. JOHN'S ROAD
(Away)

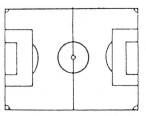

WATLING STREET

MAIN STAND

Travelling Supporters Information:
Routes: From Town Centre/Railway Station proceed up East Hill and take 3rd right into Watling Street via Dartford Tunnel A2 Dartford turn-off — floodlights visible from roundabout — Princes Hotel. From Kent Coast: A2/M2 turn-off for Greenhithe/Stone left at roundabout and right at traffic lights into Watling Street.

MANCHESTER CITY FC

Founded: 1887	**Record Attendance:** 84,569 (3/3/34)
Turned Professional: 1887	**Colours:** Shirts — Sky Blue
Limited Company: 1894	Shorts — White
Admitted to League: 1892	**Telephone No.:** (061) 226 1191
Former Name(s): Ardwick FC (1887-94)	**Ticket Information:**
Nickname: 'Citizens' 'City' 'Blues'	**Pitch Size:** 117 x 76yds
Ground: Maine Road, Moss Side,	**Ground Capacity:** 43,698
Manchester M14 7WN	**Seating Capacity:** 24,338

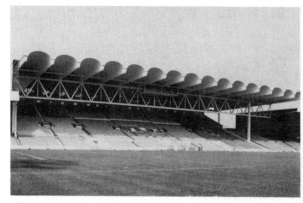

GENERAL INFORMATION
Supporters Club Administrator: Frank Horrocks
Address: Manchester City Supporter's Club Maine Road, Manchester M14 7WN
Telephone Number: (061) 226 5047
Car Parking: Kippax Street Car Park, Street Parking & Local Schools
Coach Parking: Platt Lane
Nearest Railway Station: Manchester Piccadilly (2½ miles)
Nearest Bus Station: Chorlton Street
Club Shop:
Opening Times: Weekdays 9.30 -5.00, match days 9.30-5.30 p.m.
Telephone No.: (061) 226 4824
Postal Sales: Yes
Nearest Police Station: Platt Lane, Moss Side, Manchester
Police Force: Greater Manchester
Police Telephone Number: (061) 872 5050

GROUND INFORMATION
Away Supporters' Entrances: Turnstiles 55, 56, 57 & 58. Platt Lane
Away Supporters' Sections: Platt Lane Stand (Seating)
Family Facilities: Location of Stand: Main Stand (Platt Lane End)
Capacity of Stand: 9,000
Away Families: Yes (Advance Bookings)

DISABLED SUPPORTERS INFORMATION
Wheelchairs: Accommodated in Disabled Section (in front of family stand)
Disabled Toilets: Yes
The Blind: No Special Facilities

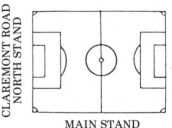

Travelling Supporters Information:
Routes: From North & West: Take M61 & M63 exit Juntion 9 following signs to Manchester (A5103). Turn right at crossroads (2¾ miles) into Claremont Road. After ¼ mile turn right into Maine Road; From South: Exit M6 Junction 19 to A556 and M56 Junction 3 following signs to Manchester (A5103) (then as North); From East: Exit M62 Junction 17 and take A56 to A57 (M) (Manchester Airport) signs. Then follow Birmingham signs to A5103 and turn left into Claremont Road (1¼ miles) (then as North).

MANCHESTER UNITED FC

Founded: 1878	**Record Attendance:** 76,962 (25/3/39)
Turned Professional: 1902	**Colours:** Shirts — Red
Limited Company: 1907	Shorts — White
Admitted to League: 1892	**Telephone No.:** (061) 872 1661
Former Name(s): Newton Heath LYR FC	**Ticket Information:** (061) 872 0199
(1878-1892); Newton Heath FC (1892-1902)	**Pitch Size:** 116 x 76yds
Nickname: 'Red Devils'	**Ground Capacity:** 46,475
Ground: Old Trafford, Warwick Road	**Seating Capacity:** 29,813
North, Manchester M16 ORA	

GENERAL INFORMATION
Supporters Club Administrator: Barry Moorhouse
Address: c/o Club
Telephone Number: (061) 872 5208
Car Parking: Lancashire Cricket Ground (1,200 cars) & White City (900 cars)
Coach Parking: By Police Direction
Nearest Railway Station: At Ground
Nearest Bus Station: Aytoun Street, Manchester
Club Shop:
Opening Times: Weekdays & match days 9.30-5.00 p.m.
Telephone No.: (061) 872 3398
Postal Sales: Yes
Nearest Police Station: Talbot Road, Stretford, (½ mile)
Police Force: Greater Manchester
Police Telephone Number: (061) 872 5050

GROUND INFORMATION
Away Supporters' Entrances: Turnstiles 94-98 Scoreboard End
Away Supporters' Sections: Scoreboard End
Family Facilities: Location of Stand: CNR Railway Side & Old Trafford End
Capacity of Stand: 2,007
Away Families: Yes — By Prior Arrangements

DISABLED SUPPORTERS INFORMATION
Wheelchairs: Accommodated in Disabled Section in front of 'L' Stand (Limited Number by prior notice)
Disabled Toilets: Yes
The Blind: Commentaries available

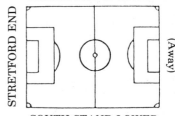

UNITED ROAD STAND
NORTH STAND LOWER
STRETFORD END
WARWICK ROAD NORTH
OLD TRAFFORD END
(Away)
SOUTH STAND LOWER
RAILWAY   FAMILY
MAIN STAND   STAND

Travelling Supporters Information:
Routes: From North & West: Take M61 to M63 and exit Junction 4 and follow Manchester signs (A5081). Turn right (2½ miles) into Warwick Road; From South: Exit M6 Junction 19 take Stockport (A556) then Altrincham (A56). From Altrincham follow Manchester signs, turn left into Warwick Road (6 miles); From East: Exit M62 Junction 17 then A56 to Manchester. Follow signs South then Chester (Chester Road), turn right into Warwick Road (2 miles).

MANSFIELD TOWN FC

Founded: 1891	**Record Attendance:** 24,467 (10/1/53)
Turned Professional: 1905	**Colours:** Shirts — Amber/Blue Trim
Limited Company: 1905	Shorts — Royal Blue/Amber Trim
Admitted to League: 1931	**Telephone No.:** (0623) 23567
Former Name(s): Mansfield Wesleyans FC	**Ticket Information:** (0623) 23567
(1891/1905)	**Pitch Size:** 115 x 72yds
Nickname: 'Stags'	**Ground Capacity:** 10,057
Ground: Field Mill Ground, Quarry Lane,	**Seating Capacity:** 3,448
Mansfield, Notts	

GENERAL INFORMATION

Supporters Club Administrator: Miss M. Brown
Address: 44 Portland Avenue, Annesley Woodhouse, Nottinghamshire
Telephone Number: (0623) 754 1823
Car Parking: Large Car Park at Ground
Coach Parking: Adjacent
Nearest Railway Station: Mansfield Alfreton Parkway — 9 miles (no public transport)
Nearest Bus Station: Mansfield
Club Shop:
Opening Times: Weekdays & match days 9.00-5.00
Telephone No.: (0623) 658070
Postal Sales: Yes
Nearest Police Station: Mansfield (¼ mile)
Police Force: Nottinghamshire
Police Telephone Number: (0623) 22622

GROUND INFORMATION

Away Supporters' Entrances: Quarry Lane Turnstiles
Away Supporters' Sections: Quarry Lane End (Open)
Family Facilities: Location of Stand: Chad Family Stand
Capacity of Stand: 1,130
Away Families: None

DISABLED SUPPORTERS INFORMATION

Wheelchairs: Accommodated — North End, West Stand
Disabled Toilets: Yes (from October 1991)
The Blind: No special facilities

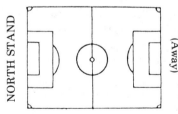

BISHOP STREET STAND

NORTH STAND / QUARRY LANE (Away)

(Disabled)   WEST STAND

Travelling Supporters Information:

Routes: From North: Exit M1 Junction 29, take A617 to Mansfield. After 6¼ miles turn right at Leisure Centre into Rosemary Street. Carry on to Quarry Lane and turn right. From South & West: Exit M1 Junction 28, take A38 to Mansfield, after 6½ miles turn right at crossroads into Belvedere Street, turn right after ¼ mile into Quarry Lane. From East: Take A617 to Rainworth, turn right at crossroads (3 miles) into Windsor Road and right at end into Nottingham Road, then left into Quarry Lane.

MIDDLESBROUGH FC

Founded: 1876
Turned Professional: 1889
Limited Company: 1892
Admitted to League: 1899
Former Name(s): None
Nickname: 'Boro'
Ground: Ayresome Park, Middlesbrough
Cleveland TS1 4PB

Record Attendance: 53,596 (27/12/49)
Colours: Shirts — Red with White Yoke
Shorts — White
Telephone No.: (0642) 819659
Ticket Information: (0642) 815996
Pitch Size: 114 x 73yds
Ground Capacity: 26,385
Seating Capacity: 12,585

GENERAL INFORMATION
Supporters Club Administrator: Andy Hyams
Address: c/o Club
Telephone Number: (0642) 819659
Car Parking: Street Parking
Coach Parking: By Police Direction
Nearest Railway Station: Middlesbrough (1 mile)
Nearest Bus Station: Middlesbrough
Club Shop:
Opening Times: Monday-Friday 9.30-5.00 + Saturday Matchdays
Telephone No.: (0642) 826664
Postal Sales: Yes
Nearest Police Station: Dunning Street, Middlesbrough (1 mile)
Police Force: Cleveland
Police Telephone Number: (0642) 248184

GROUND INFORMATION
Away Supporters' Entrances: Turnstiles — South East corner
Away Supporters' Sections: South East corner (Open & Seating)
Family Facilities: Location of Stand: North Stand
Capacity of Stand: 1,511
Away Families: None

DISABLED SUPPORTERS INFORMATION
Wheelchairs: Accommodated in North-East Corner
Disabled Toilets: None
The Blind: Commentaries — North Stand

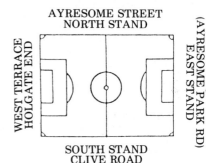

Travelling Supporters Information:
Routes: From North: Take A19 across Tees Bridge and join A66 (¼ mile). Take 3rd exit at roundabout (½ mile) into Heywood Street, and left into Ayresome Street at end. From South: Take A1 & A19 to junction with A66, take 4th exit at roundabout (½ mile) into Heywood Street (then as North). From West: Take A66 then 1½ miles after Teesside Park Racecourse take 4th exit at roundabout into Ayresome Street.

MILLWALL FC

Founded: 1885	**Record Attendance:** 48,672 (20/2/37)
Turned Professional: 1893	**Colours:** Shirts — Blue
Limited Company: 1894	Shorts — White
Admitted to League: 1920	**Telephone No.:** (071) 639 3143
Former Name(s): Millwall Rovers FC (1885	**Ticket Information:** (071) 639 3143
/1893); Milwall Athletic FC (1893/1925)	**Pitch Size:** 112 x 74yds
Nickname: 'Lions'	**Ground Capacity:** 22,000
Ground: The Den, Cold Blow Lane, New	**Seating Capacity:** 2,690
Cross, London SE14 5RH	

GENERAL INFORMATION
Supporters Club Administrator: None
Address: —
Telephone Number: —
Car Parking: Ilderton Road car park
Coach Parking: Ilderton Road
Nearest Railway Station: New Cross Gate (½ mile)
Nearest Tube Station: New Cross Gate (½ mile)
Club Shop:
Opening Times: Daily 9.00-5.00
Telephone No.: (071) 639 4590
Postal Sales: Yes
Nearest Police Station: Deptford/Lewisham (1 mile)
Police Force: Metropolitan
Police Telephone Number: (071) 679 9217

GROUND INFORMATION
Away Supporters' Entrances: Ilderton Road (away fans must buy tickets from their own club)
Away Supporters' Sections: Ilderton Road end (covered)
Family Facilities: Location of Stand: North Stand
Capacity of Stand: —
Away Families: Yes - by arrangement
DISABLED SUPPORTERS INFORMATION
Wheelchairs: Accommodated — Disabled Section South Stand
Disabled Toilets: Yes
The Blind: No special facilities

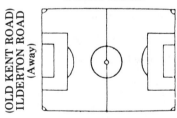

Travelling Supporters Information:
Routes: From North: Follow City signs from M1/A1 then signs for Shoreditch and Whitechapel. Follow signs Ring Road, Dover, cross over Tower Bridge, take 1st exit at roundabout (1 mile) on to A2. From Elephant and Castle take A2 (Old Kent Road) into New Kent Road and turn left (after 4 miles) at Canterbury Arms pub into Ilderton Road (car park on right). Do NOT take routes into Cold Blow Lane. From South: Take A20 and A21 following signs to London. At New Cross follow signs for City, Westminster into Kender Street and follow into Avonley Road (then as North). From East: Take A2 to New Cross (then as South). From West: From M4 and M3 follow South Circular (A205) following signs for Clapham, City A3 then Camberwell, New Cross and then Rochester (A202). In ¾ mile turn left into Kender Street (then as South).

NEWCASTLE UNITED FC

Founded: 1882	**Record Attendance:** 68,386 (3/9/30)
Turned Professional: 1889	**Colours:** Shirts — Black and White stripes
Limited Company: 1890	Shorts — Black
Admitted to League: 1893	**Telephone No.:** (091) 232 8361
Former Name(s): Newcastle East End FC	**Ticket Information:** (091) 261 1571
(1882-92); Became 'United' when amalg-	**Pitch Size:** 115 x 75yds
amated with Newcastle West End FC	**Ground Capacity:** 33,530
Nickname: 'Magpies'	**Seating Capacity:** 11,413

Ground: St. James Park, Newcastle-Upon-Tyne, NE1 4ST

GROUND INFORMATION
Away Supporters' Entrances: Turnstiles 45 & 46
Away Supporters' Sections: Leazes End 'H' Paddock (Open)
Family Facilities: Location of Stand: East Stand Paddock (seats) (members only)
Capacity of Stand: 843 seated
Away Families: By prior arrangement

DISABLED SUPPORTERS INFORMATION
Wheelchairs: Accommodated in Disabled Section (Leazes Terrace West)
Disabled Toilets: Yes
The Blind: Facilities for 20 Blind supporters

GENERAL INFORMATION
Supporters Club Administrator: Kenneth Mullen
Address: 7 Prudhoe Place, Haymarket, Newcastle-Upon-Tyne
Telephone Number: (091) 232 2473
Car Parking: Leazes Car Park & Street Parking
Coach Parking: Leazes Car Park
Nearest Railway Station: Newcastle Central (½ mile)
Nearest Bus Station: Gallowgate (¼ mile)
Club Shop:
Opening Times: Monday-Saturday 9.00-5.00, Matchdays 9.00-5.30
Telephone No.: (091) 261 6357
Postal Sales: Yes
Also in Metrocentre, Gateshead. Monday — Saturday 10.00 — 8.00
Telephone No.: (091) 232 4080
Nearest Police Station: Market Street Newcastle
Police Force: Northumbria
Police Telephone Number: (091) 232 3451

Travelling Supporters Information:
Routes: From North: Follow A1 into Newcastle, then Hexham signs into Percy Street. Turn right into Leaze Park Road; From South: Take A1M, then after Birtley Granada Services take A69 Gateshead Western Bypass (bear left on motorway). Follow Airport signs for approximately 3 miles then take A692 (Newcastle) sign, crossing the Redheugh Bridge. At roundabout take 3rd exit (Blenheim Street). Proceed over two sets of traffic light crossing Westmorland Road and Westgate Road. Turn left into Bath Lane. Over traffic lights to next roundabout and take third exit into Barrack Road; From West: Take A69 towards City Centre. Pass Newcastle General Hospital. At traffic lights immediately after hospital turn left into Brighton Grove and after 70 yards turn right into Stanhope Street. Proceed into Barrack Road.

NORTHAMPTON TOWN FC

Founded: 1897	**Record Attendance:** 24,523 (23/4/66)
Turned Professional: 1901	**Colours:** Shirts — Claret with Maroon Zig
Limited Company: 1901	Zag Shorts — White with Claret Zig Zag
Admitted to League: 1920	**Telephone No.:** (0604) 234100
Former Name(s): None	**Ticket Information:** (0604) 234100
Nickname: 'Cobblers'	**Pitch Size:** 112 x 75yds
Ground: County Ground, Abingdon	**Ground Capacity:** 11,682
Avenue, Northampton NN1 4PS	**Seating Capacity:** 360

GENERAL INFORMATION
Supporters Club Administrator: Alec Smith
Address: c/o Club
Telephone Number: (0604) 842636
Car Parking: Street Parking
Coach Parking: Abingdon Park
Nearest Railway Station: Northampton Castle
Nearest Bus Station: Greyfriars
Club Shop:
Opening Times: Weekdays — office hours matchdays 9.30-5.00
Telephone No.: (0604) 234100
Postal Sales: Yes
Nearest Police Station: Cambell Square, Northampton
Police Force: Northants
Police Telephone Number: (0604) 33221

GROUND INFORMATION
Away Supporters' Entrances: Abingdon Avenue
Away Supporters' Sections: Spion Kop
Family Facilities: Location of Stand: Abingdon Avenue side
Capacity of Stand: 360
Away Families: None

DISABLED SUPPORTERS INFORMATION
Wheelchairs: Accommodated on Cricket pitch side
Disabled Toilets: None
The Blind: No Special Facilities

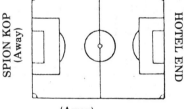

(CRICKET PITCH SIDE)
WANTAGE ROAD

SPION KOP (Away) — HOTEL END

(Away)
ABINGDON AVENUE

Travelling Supporters Information:
Routes: From North & West: Take A45 into Northampton and follow signs for Kettering (A43) into Kettering Road. After almost 1 mile turn right into Abingdon Avenue. From East: Take A45 to Wilby. After 5¼ miles continue across roundabout and in 2½ miles turn right over crossroads into Abingdon Avenue. From South: Exit M1 junction 15 following signs for Kettering (A43) into Kettering Road (then as North).

NORWICH CITY FC

Founded: 1905
Turned Professional: 1905
Limited Company: 1905
Admitted to League: 1920
Former Name(s): None
Nickname: 'Canaries'
Ground: Carrow Road, Norwich, NR1 1JE
(Information Line 0603 121514)

Record Attendance: 43,984 (30/3/63)
Colours: Shirts — Yellow
          Shorts — Green
Telephone No.: (0603) 612131
Ticket Information: (0603) 761661
Pitch Size: 114 x 74yds
Ground Capacity: 24,260
Seating Capacity: 11,285

GENERAL INFORMATION
Supporters Club Administrator: Kevan Platt
Address: Club Canary, Carrow Road, Norwich
Telephone Number: (0603) 761125
Car Parking: City Centre Car Parks (nearby)
Coach Parking: Lower Clarence Road
Nearest Railway Station: Norwich (½ mile)
Nearest Bus Station: Surrey Street, Norwich
Club Shop: (In City Stand)
Opening Times: Weekdays & matchdays 9.00-4.45
Telephone No.: (0603) 761125
Postal Sales: Yes
Nearest Police Station: Bethel Street, Norwich (1 mile)
Police Force: Norfolk
Police Telephone Number: (0603) 621212

GROUND INFORMATION
Away Supporters' Entrances: Turnstiles 4-12
Away Supporters' Sections: Barclay Stand (Covered)
Family Facilities: Location of Stand: South Stand
Capacity of Stand: 1,688
Away Families: Yes

DISABLED SUPPORTERS INFORMATION
Wheelchairs: Accommodated in Disabled Section (glazed & heated — situated South Stand/River End Corner)
Disabled Toilets: Yes
The Blind: No Special Facilities

Travelling Supporters Information:
Routes: From North: Take A140 to junction with Ring Road and follow signs Yarmouth (A47) after 3½ miles turn right at 'T' junction, turn left ½ mile into Carrow Road; From South & West: Take A11/A140 into Norwich and follow signs Yarmouth to Ring Road for Carrow Road; From East: Take A47 into Norwich then left into Ring Road for Carrow Road

NOTTINGHAM FOREST FC

Founded: 1865	**Record Attendance:** 49,945 (28/10/67)
Turned Professional: 1889	**Colours:** Shirts — Red
Limited Company: 1982	Shorts — White
Admitted to League: 1892	**Telephone No.:** (0602) 822202
Former Name(s): None	**Ticket Information:** (0602) 813801
Nickname: 'Reds' 'Forest'	**Pitch Size:** 115 x 78yds
Ground: City Ground, Nottingham	**Ground Capacity:** 31,920
NG2 5FJ	**Seating Capacity:** 15,114

GENERAL INFORMATION
Supporters Club Administrator: Mr. B. Tewson
Address: c/o Club
Telephone Number: (0602) 822202
Car Parking: East Car Park (300 cars) & Street Parking
Coach Parking: East Car Park, Meadow Lane
Nearest Railway Station: Nottingham Midland (½ mile)
Nearest Bus Station: Victoria Street /Broadmarsh Centre
Club Shop:
Opening Times: Weekdays 9.00-5.00, Matchdays 9.00-3.00
Telephone No.: (0602) 820444
Postal Sales: Yes
Nearest Police Station: Rectory Road, West Bridgford (1 mile)
Police Force: Nottinghamshire
Police Telephone Number: (0602) 481888

GROUND INFORMATION
Away Supporters' Entrances: Via East Car Park
Away Supporters' Sections: T. Block Executive Stand & Visitors Terrace
Family Facilities: Location of Stand: Blocks G & Q Trent End
Capacity of Stand: —
Away Families: None

DISABLED SUPPORTERS INFORMATION
Wheelchairs: Limited Accommodation in Disabled Section (in front of executive stand)
Disabled Toilets: Yes
The Blind: No Special Facilities

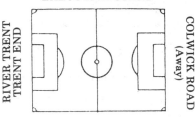

Travelling Supporters Information:
Routes: From North: Exit M1 junction 26 following Nottingham signs (A610) then Melton Mowbray and Trent Bridge (A606) signs. Cross River Trent, left into Radcliffe Road then left into Colwick Road; From South: Exit M1 junction 24 following signs Nottingham (South) to Trent Bridge. Turn right into Radcliffe Road then left into Colwick Road; From East: Take A52 to West Bridgford, turn right into Colwick Road; From West: Take A52 into Nottingham following signs Melton Mowbray and Trent Bridge, cross River Trent (then as North).

NOTTS COUNTY FC

Founded: 1862 (Oldest in League)
Turned Professional: 1885
Limited Company: 1888
Admitted to League: 1888 (Founder)
Former Name(s): None
Nickname: 'Magpies'
Ground: Meadow Lane, Nottingham
NG2 3HJ

Record Attendance: 47,301 (12/3/55)
Colours: Shirts — Black & White stripes
Amber Sleeve & Trim   Shorts — Black
Telephone No.: (0602) 861155
Ticket Information: (0602) 861155
Pitch Size: 117 x 76yds
Ground Capacity: 20,834
Seating Capacity: 3,884

GENERAL INFORMATION
Supporters Club Administrator: P. Dennis
Address: c/o Club
Telephone Number: (0602) 866802
Car Parking: British Waterways, Meadow Lane
Coach Parking: British Waterways, Meadow Lane
Nearest Railway Station: Nottingham Midland (½ mile)
Nearest Bus Station: Broadmarsh Centre
Club Shop:
Opening Times: Weekdays & Matchdays 9.00-5.00
Telephone No.: (0602) 861155
Postal Sales: Yes
Nearest Police Station: Station Street, Nottingham
Police Force: Nottinghamshire
Police Telephone Number: (0602) 481888

GROUND INFORMATION
Away Supporters' Entrances: Cattle Market Corner, County Road
Away Supporters' Sections: Cattle Market Corner, County Road Stand (Some covered)
Family Facilities: Location of Stand: Meadow Lane End & Kop End Main Stand
Capacity of Stand: 2,260
Away Families: None

DISABLED SUPPORTERS INFORMATION
Wheelchairs: Accommodated in Disabled Section County Road/Meadow Lane End Corner
Disabled Toilets: None
The Blind: No Special Facilities

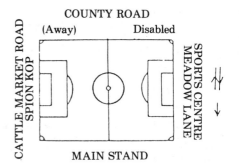

Travelling Supporters Information:
Routes: From North: Exit M1 junction 26 following Nottingham signs (A610) then Melton Mowbray and Trent Bridge (A606) signs. Before River Trent turn left into Meadow Lane; From South: Exit M1 junction 24 following signs Nottingham (South) to Trent Bridge, cross River and follow one-way system to the right, then turn left and right at traffic lights then second right into Meadow Lane; From East: Take A52 to West Bridgford/Trent Bridge, cross River and follow one-way system to the right then turn left and right at traffic lights, then second right into Meadow Lane; From West: Take A52 into Nottingham following signs Melton Mowbray and Trent Bridge, before River Trent turn left into Meadow Lane.

OLDHAM ATHLETIC FC

Founded: 1894
Turned Professional: 1899
Limited Company: 1906
Admitted to League: 1907
Former Name(s): Pine Villa FC (1894-99)
Nickname: 'Latics'
Ground: Boundary Park, Oldham
OL1 2PA

Record Attendance: 47,671 (25/1/30)
Colours: Shirts — Blue
Shorts — Blue
Telephone No.: (061) 624 4972 (24 hrs)
Pitch Size: 110 x 74yds
Ground Capacity: 18,500
Seating Capacity: 6,600

GENERAL INFORMATION
Supporters Club Administrator: Alan Hardy
Address: c/o Club
Telephone Number: (061) 627 1802
Car Parking: Lookers Stand Car Park (1000 cars)
Coach Parking: At Ground
Nearest Railway Station: Oldham Werneth (1½ miles)
Nearest Bus Station: Oldham Mumps (2 miles)
Club Shop:
Opening Times: Mondays-Saturdays 9.00-5.00 p.m.
Telephone No.: (061) 652 0966
Postal Sales: Yes
Nearest Police Station: Chadderton
Police Force: Greater Manchester
Police Telephone Number: (061) 624 0444

GROUND INFORMATION
Away Supporters' Entrances: Rochdale Road turnstiles & Ashdene & Windsor turnstile 14
Away Supporters' Sections: Rochdale Road End standing / Ashdene and Windsor Stand White block (seating)
Family Facilities: Location of Stand: Lookers Stand
Capacity of Stand: 1,500
Away Families: None

DISABLED SUPPORTERS INFORMATION
Wheelchairs: Accommodated in Disabled Section in Lookers Stand
Disabled Toilets: Yes
The Blind: Commentaries available

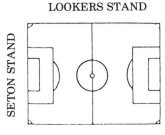

Travelling Supporters Information:
Routes: From All Parts: Exit M62 junction 20 and take A627M to junction with A664. Take 1st exit at roundabout on to Broadway, then 1st right into Hilbre Avenue which leads to car park.

OXFORD UNITED FC

Founded: 1893
Turned Professional: 1949
Limited Company: 1949
Admitted to League: 1962
Former Name(s): Headington United FC (1893/1960)
Nickname: 'U's'
Ground: Manor Ground, London Road, Headington, Oxford OX3 7RS

Record Attendance: 22,730 (29/2/64)
Colours: Shirts — Yellow with Navy trim
Shorts — Navy with Yellow trim
Telephone No.: (0865) 61503
Ticket Information: (0865) 61503
Pitch Size: 110 x 75yds
Ground Capacity: 11,622
Seating Capacity: 2,777

GENERAL INFORMATION
Supporters Club Administrator: Gary Whiting
Address: c/o The Club
Telephone Number: (0865) 63063
Car Parking: Street Parking
Coach Parking: Headley Way
Nearest Railway Station: Oxford (3 miles)
Nearest Bus Station: Queen's Lane (2 miles)
Club Shop: 67 London Road, Headington (2 minutes walk)
Opening Times: Mon-Sat 9.30-5.30 (closes 2.00 matchdays)
Telephone No.: (0865) 61503
Postal Sales: Yes
Nearest Police Station: Cowley (2 miles)
Police Force: Thames Valley
Police Telephone Number: (0865) 777501

GROUND INFORMATION
Away Supporters' Entrances: Cuckoo Lane Turnstiles 5-11
Away Supporters' Sections: Cuckoo Lane Stand
Family Facilities: Location of Stand: Beech Road Side (Members only)
Capacity of Stand: 162 uncovered seating, 170 covered seating
Away Families: None

DISABLED SUPPORTERS INFORMATION
Wheelchairs: Accommodated in Disabled section (limited number — apply in advance)
Disabled Toilets: Yes
The Blind: No Special facilities

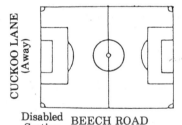

(Members Only)
OSLER ROAD

CUCKOO LANE (Away)

LONDON ROAD

Disabled Section
BEECH ROAD
(Members Only)

Travelling Supporters Information:
Routes: From North: Follow signs Ring Road, London (A40), take 4th exit at roundabout towards Headington, turn right (¾ mile) into Sandfield Road, then right into Beech Road; From South: Take A34 to Bypass London (A4142), take 1st exit at roundabout towards Headington (then as North); From East: Take M40 to A40, take 2nd exit at roundabout to Headington (then as North); From West: Take A420 to Oxford and follow signs London along Headington Road, turn left (2 miles) into Sandfield Road, then right into Beech Road.
Bus Services: Service 1 Railway Station to Queens Lane, Service 2 ground.

PETERBOROUGH UNITED FC

Founded: 1923	**Record Attendance:** 30,096 (20/2/65)
Turned Professional: 1934	**Colours:** Shirts — Blue
Limited Company: 1934	Shorts — White
Admitted to League: 1960	**Telephone No.:** (0733) 63947
Former Name(s): Peterborough & Fletton	**Ticket Information:** (0733) 63947
United FC (1923-34)	**Pitch Size:** 112 x 76yds
Nickname: 'Posh'	**Ground Capacity:** 16,414
Ground: London Road, Peterborough,	**Seating Capacity:** 3,500
Cambs PE2 8AL	

GENERAL INFORMATION
Supporters Club Administrator: Brian Davies
Address: c/o Club
Telephone Number: —
Car Parking: Ample Parking at Ground
Coach Parking: Rear of Ground
Nearest Railway Station: Peterborough (1 mile)
Nearest Bus Station: Peterborough (¼ mile)
Club Shop:
Opening Times: Monday-Friday 9.00-5.00 (Closes for Lunch 1.00-2.00)
Telephone No.: (0733) 63947
Postal Sales: Yes
Nearest Police Station: Bridge Street, Peterborough (5 minutes walk)
Police Force: Cambridgeshire
Police Telephone Number: (0733) 63232

GROUND INFORMATION
Away Supporters' Entrances: Turnstile A Moys End
Away Supporters' Sections: Moys End (Covered) (Standing) — Block A Seating
Family Facilities: Location of Stand: Marwin Corner — D Stand
Capacity of Stand: 3,500
Away Families: None

DISABLED SUPPORTERS INFORMATION
Wheelchairs: Accommodated in Disabled Section
Disabled Toilets: None
The Blind: No Special Facilities

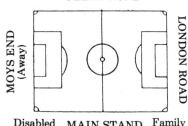

GLEBE ROAD

MOYS END (Away)

LONDON ROAD

Disabled Area   MAIN STAND   Family Corner

Travelling Supporters Information:
Routes: From North & West: Take A1 then A47 into Town Centre, follow Whittlesey signs across river into London Road; From East: Take A47 into Town Centre (then as North); From South: Take A1 then A15 Road into London Road.

PLYMOUTH ARGYLE FC

Founded: 1886
Turned Professional: 1903
Limited Company: 1903
Admitted to League: 1920
Former Name(s): Argyle FC (1886/1903)
Nickname: 'Pilgrims' 'Argyle'
Ground: Home Park, Plymouth,
PL2 3DQ

Record Attendance: 43,596 (10/10/36)
Colours: Shirts — Green & White Stripes
Shorts — Black
Telephone No.: (0752) 562561
Ticket Information: (0752) 562561
Pitch Size: 112 x 72yds
Ground Capacity: 24,000
Seating Capacity: 3,099

GENERAL INFORMATION
Supporters Club Administrator: S. Rendell
Address: c/o Club
Telephone Number: (0752) 561041
Car Parking: Car Park (1,000 cars) Adjacent
Coach Parking: Central Car Park
Nearest Railway Station: Plymouth North Road
Nearest Bus Station: Bretonside Plymouth
Club Shop:
Opening Times: Monday-Saturday 9.00-5.00
Telephone No.: (0752) 558292
Postal Sales: Yes
Nearest Police Station: Devonport (1 mile)
Police Force: Devon & Cornwall
Police Telephone Number: (0752) 701188

GROUND INFORMATION
Away Supporters' Entrances: Barn Park End Turnstiles
Away Supporters' Sections: Barn Park End (Open)
Family Facilities: Location of Stand: Devonport End of Grandstand
Capacity of Stand: 3,099

DISABLED SUPPORTERS INFORMATION
Wheelchairs: Accommodated in Disabled Section
Disabled Toilets: Devonport End
The Blind: Commentaries Available

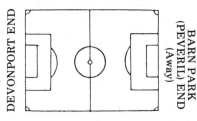

Travelling Supporters Information:
Routes: From All Parts: Take A38 to Tavistock Road (A386), then branch left following signs Plymouth (A386), continue for 1¼ miles — car park on left.

PORTSMOUTH FC

Founded: 1898	**Record Attendance:** 51,385 (26/2/49)
Turned Professional: 1898	**Colours:** Shirts — Blue
Limited Company: 1898	Shorts — White
Admitted to League: 1920	**Telephone No.:** (0705) 731204
Former Name(s): None	**Ticket Information:** (0705) 750825
Nickname: 'Pompey'	**Pitch Size:** 116 x 73yds
Ground: Fratton Park, 57 Frogmore Road,	**Ground Capacity:** 26,300
Portsmouth, Hants, PO4 8RA	**Seating Capacity:** 7,000

GENERAL INFORMATION
Supporters Club Administrator: —
Address: c/o Club
Telephone Number: —
Car Parking: Street Parking
Coach Parking: By Police Direction
Nearest Railway Station: Fratton (Adjacent)
Nearest Bus Station: Eastney
Club Shop:
Opening Times: Monday-Saturday 9.00-5.00
Telephone No.: (0705) 738358
Postal Sales: Yes
Nearest Police Station: Southsea
Police Force: Hampshire
Police Telephone Number: (0705) 321111

GROUND INFORMATION
Away Supporters' Entrances: Aspley Road — Milton Road side
Away Supporters' Sections: Aspley Road End (Open)
Family Facilities: Location of Stand: 2 — South Enclosure, Carisbrooke Road & 'G' Section, Milton Road
Capacity of Stand: 3,300 (S); 3,200 (N)

DISABLED SUPPORTERS INFORMATION
Wheelchairs: Accommodated in Disabled Section
Disabled Toilets: Yes
The Blind: Commentaries Available

MILTON ROAD
NORTH STAND

FROGMORE ROAD
FRATTON END

ASPLEY ROAD
(MILTON END)
(Away)

SOUTH STAND
CARISBROOKE ROAD

Travelling Supporters Information:
Routes: From North & West: Take M27 and M275 to end then take 2nd exit at roundabout and in ¼ mile turn right at 'T' junction into London Road (A2047), in 1¼ mile cross railway bridge and turn left into Goldsmith Avenue. After ½ mile turn left into Frogmore Road; From East: Take A27 following Southsea signs (A2030). Turn left at roundabout (3 miles) into A288, then right into Priory Crescent and next right into Carisbrooke Road.

PORT VALE FC

Founded: 1876	**Record Attendance:** 50,000 (20/2/60)
Turned Professional: 1885	**Colours:** Shirts — White
Limited Company: 1911	Shorts — Black
Admitted to League: 1892	**Telephone No.:** (0782) 814134
Former Name(s): Burslem Port Vale FC	**Ticket Information:** (0782) 814134
(1876/1913)	**Pitch Size:** 118 x 75yds
Nickname: 'Valiants'	**Ground Capacity:** 20,111
Ground: Vale Park, Burslem, Stoke-on-	**Seating Capacity:** 9,421
Trent, ST6 1AW	

GENERAL INFORMATION
Supporters Club Administrator: G. Wakefield
Address: c/o Club
Telephone Number: (0538) 266228
Car Parking: Car Parks at Ground
Coach Parking: Hamil Road Car Park
Nearest Railway Station: Longport, Stoke
Nearest Bus Station: Burslem
Club Shop:
Opening Times: Monday-Saturday 9.00 — 5.30 p.m.
Telephone No.: (0782) 824355
Postal Sales: Yes
Nearest Police Station: Burslem
Police Force: Staffordshire
Police Telephone Number: (0782) 577114

GROUND INFORMATION
Away Supporters' Entrances: Hamil Road turnstiles
Away Supporters' Sections: Hamil Road End & Railway Stand — Block C
Family Facilities: Location of Stand: New Family Stand
Capacity of Stand: 1,000
Away Families: Accommodated

DISABLED SUPPORTERS INFORMATION
Wheelchairs: Accommodated in Disabled Section
Disabled Toilets: Yes
The Blind: Commentaries may be available by prior arrangement

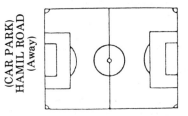

Travelling Supporters Information:
Routes: From North: Exit M6 junction 16 and follow Stoke signs (A500). Branch left off the A500 at the exit signposted Tunstall and take 1st exit at roundabout onto A50. Turn right ¼ mile into Newcastle Street and at end cross into Moorland Road. Then turn left into Hamil Road; From South and West: Exit M6 junction 15 and take A5006 and A500, after 6¼ miles branch left (then as North); From East: Take A50 or A52 into Stoke following Burslem signs into Waterloo Road, turn right at Burslem crossroads into Moorland Road (then as North).

PRESTON NORTH END FC

Founded: 1881
Turned Professional: 1885
Limited Company: 1893
Admitted to League: 1888
Former Name(s): Preston Nelson FC (1881/82)
Nickname: 'Lilywhites', 'North End'
Ground: Lowthorpe Road, Deepdale, Preston PR1 6RU

Record Attendance: 42,684 (23/4/38)
Colours: Shirts — White
Shorts — Blue
Telephone No.: (0772) 795919
Ticket Information: (0772) 709170 (answerphone)
Pitch Size: 110 x 72yds
Ground Capacity: 15,120
Seating Capacity: 3,000

GENERAL INFORMATION
Supporters Club Administrator: Maureen Robinson
Address: 40 Southgate, Fulwood, Preston
Telephone Number: (0772) 774005
Car Parking: West Stand car park (600 cars)
Coach Parking: West Stand car park
Nearest Railway Station: Preston (2 miles)
Nearest Bus Station: Preston (1 mile)
Club Shop:
Opening Times: Weekdays 9.00-5.00, Matchdays 11.00-3.00
Telephone No.: (0772) 795465
Postal Sales: Yes
Nearest Police Station: Lawson Street, Preston (1 mile)
Police Force: Lancashire
Police Telephone Number: (0772) 203203

GROUND INFORMATION
Away Supporters' Entrances: Turnstiles 3-11 Deepdale Road (Standing): 13-14 (Seats)
Away Supporters' Sections: Town end (covered), West Stand (seats)
Family Facilities: Location of Stand: West Stand
Capacity of Stand: 300
Away Families: Possibly, by prior arrangement

DISABLED SUPPORTERS INFORMATION
Wheelchairs: Accommodated in Disabled Section in West Stand Paddock
Disabled Toilets: Yes
The Blind: No Special Facilities

DEEPDALE ROAD
WEST STAND

TOWN END (Away)

HOLLINS ROAD
FULWOOD END

PAVILION STAND
LOWTHORPE ROAD

Travelling Supporters Information:
Routes: From North: M6 then M55 to junction 1. Follow signs to Preston A6. After 2 miles turn left at the crossroads into Blackpool Road (A5085). Turn right ¾ mile into Deepdale. From South and East: Exit M6 at junction 31 and follow Preston signs (A59). Take 2nd exit at roundabout (1 mile) into Blackpool Road. Turn left (1¼ mile) into Deepdale. From West: Exit M55 junction 1 (then as North).

QUEENS PARK RANGERS FC

Founded: 1882	**Record Attendance:** 35,353 (27/4/74)
Turned Professional: 1898	**Colours:** Shirts — Blue and White Hoops
Limited Company: 1899	Shorts — White
Admitted to League: 1920	**Telephone No.:** (081) 743 0262
Former Name(s): Formed by amalgamation	**Ticket Information:** (081) 749 5744
of St. Jude's & Christchurch Rangers FC's	**Pitch Size:** 110 x 75yds
Nickname: 'Rangers' 'R's'	**Ground Capacity:** 23,480
Ground: Rangers Stadium, South Africa	**Seating Capacity:** 15,026
Road, London W12 7PA	

GENERAL INFORMATION
Supporters Club Administrator: Neil Roberts
Address: c/o Club
Telephone Number: (081) 749 6771
Car Parking: White City NCP
Coach Parking: White City
Nearest Railway Station: Shepherd's Bush
Nearest Tube Station: White City (Central)
Club Shop:
Opening Times: Mon-Sat 9.00-5.00
Telephone No.: (081) 743 0262
Postal Sales: Yes
Nearest Police Station: Uxbridge Road, Shepherds Bush (½ mile)
Police Force: Metropolitan
Police Telephone Number: (081) 741 6212

GROUND INFORMATION
Away Supporters' Entrances: South Africa Road, Turnstiles 29-34 & Ellerslie Road, Nos 35-37
Away Supporters' Sections: West End Stand (Part-covered)
Family Facilities: Location of Stand: Loftus Road Stand
Capacity of Stand: 3,152 seating
Away Families: In West End Stand

DISABLED SUPPORTERS INFORMATION
Wheelchairs: Accommodated in Wheelchair Enclosure
Disabled Toilets: None
The Blind: No Special Facilities

← ⇄

(Disabled)
ELLERSLIE ROAD STAND

LOFTUS ROAD STAND

WEST END STAND (SCHOOL)
BLOEMFONTEIN ROAD
WEST END STAND (Away)

MAIN STAND
SOUTH AFRICA ROAD

Travelling Supporters Information:
Routes: From North: Take M1 & A406 North Circular for Neasden, turn left ¾ mile (A404) following signs Harlesden, then Hammersmith, past White City Stadium and right into White City Road, then left into South Africa Road; From South: Take A206, A3 across Putney Bridge following signs to Hammersmith, then Oxford A219 to Shepherd's Bush to join A4020 following signs to Acton, in ¼ mile turn right into Loftus Road; From East: Take A12, A406 then A503 to join Ring Road follow Oxford signs to join A40(M), branch left (2 miles) to M41, 3rd exit at roundabout to A4020 (then as South); From West: Take M4 to Chiswick then A315 and A402 to Shepherd's Bush, join A4020 (then as South)

READING FC

Founded: 1871	**Record Attendance:** 33,042 (19/2/27)
Turned Professional: 1895	**Colours:** Shirts — Sky Blue with navy collars and cuffs and yellow plaquets
Limited Company: 1897	
Admitted to League: 1920	Shorts — Navy with sky blue and yellow flash
Former Name(s): Amalgamated with Hornets FC (1877) and Earley FC (1889)	**Telephone No.:** (0734) 507878
Nickname: 'Royals'	**Ticket Information:** (0734) 507878
Ground: Elm Park, Norfolk Road, Reading RG3 2EF	**Pitch Size:** 112 x 77yds
	Ground Capacity: 13,200
	Seating Capacity: 2,400

GENERAL INFORMATION
Supporters Club Administrator: B. Page
Address: c/o Club
Telephone Number: (0734) 507878
Car Parking: Car park at ground (300 cars) and street parking
Coach Parking: The Meadway
Nearest Railway Station: Reading General (2 miles)
Nearest Bus Station: Reading
Club Shop:
Opening Times: Tuesdays-Fridays & matchdays 9.00-5.00
Telephone No.: (0734) 507878
Postal Sales: Yes
Nearest Police Station: Castle Street, Reading (2 miles)
Police Force: Thames Valley
Police Telephone Number: (0734 536000

GROUND INFORMATION
Away Supporters' Entrances: Norfolk Road Turnstiles
Away Supporters' Sections: Reading End /Norfolk Road (open Terrace only)
Family Facilities: Location of Stand: Norfolk Road side 'A' stand
Capacity of Stand: 395
Away Families: By prior arrangement

DISABLED SUPPORTERS INFORMATION
Wheelchairs: Accommodated in front row 'E' Stand (prior notice required)
Disabled Toilets: Yes
The Blind: No Special Facilities

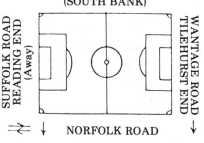

Travelling Supporters Information:
Routes: From North: Take A423, A4074 and A4155 from Oxford across railway bridge into Reading. Follow signs for Newbury (A4) into Castle Hill, then right into Tilehurst Road. Turn right after ¾ mile into Cranbury Road then left and 2nd left into Norfolk Road; From South: Take A33 into Reading and follow Newbury signs into Bath Road. Cross railway bridge and take 3rd right into Liebenrood Road. At the end turn right into Tilehurst Road then 1st left into Cranbury Road and 2nd left into Norfolk Road. From East: Exit M4 junction 10 and use A329 and A4 into Reading. Cross railway bridge (then as South); From West: Exit M4 junction 12 and take A4. After 3¼ miles turn left into Liebenrood Road (then as South).

ROCHDALE FC

Founded: 1907
Turned Professional: 1907
Limited Company: 1910
Admitted to League: 1921
Former Name(s): Rochdale Town FC
Nickname: 'The Dale'
Ground: Willbutts Lane, Spotland, Rochdale OL11 5DS

Record Attendance: 24,231 (10/12/49)
Colours: Shirts — Blue & White
Shorts — Blue & White
Telephone No.: (0706) 44648
Ticket Information: (0706) 44649
Pitch Size: 111 x 77yds
Ground Capacity: 15,000
Seating Capacity: 642

GENERAL INFORMATION
Supporters Club Administrator: R. I. Bailey
Address: c/o Club
Telephone Number: —
Car Parking: Car Park at Ground
Coach Parking: rear of Pearl Street Stand
Nearest Railway Station: Rochdale (1½ miles)
Nearest Bus Station: Town Centre (1 mile)
Club Shop:
Opening Times: Matchdays only
Telephone No.: (0706) 44648
Postal Sales: Yes
Nearest Police Station: Rochdale (1½ miles)
Police Force: Greater Manchester
Police Telephone Number: (0706) 47401

GROUND INFORMATION
Away Supporters' Entrances: Pearl Street Turnstiles
Away Supporters' Sections: Pearl St. End (Open & Covered)
Family Facilities: Location of Stand: 'B' Stand
Capacity of Stand: 120
Away Families: Yes

DISABLED SUPPORTERS INFORMATION
Wheelchairs: Accommodated on track (by prior arrangement)
Disabled Toilets: None
The Blind: No Special Facilities

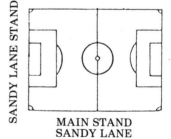

Travelling Supporters Information:
Routes: From North: Take A680 to Rochdale, watch out for right turn into Willbutts Lane; From South, East & West: Exit M62 junction 20 following Rochdale signs, take 2nd exit at 2nd roundabout (1½ miles) into Roch Valley Way and turn right (1½ miles) into Willbutts Lane.

ROTHERHAM UNITED FC

Founded: 1884	**Record Attendance:** 25,000 (13/12/52)
Turned Professional: 1905	**Colours:** Shirts — Red
Limited Company: 1920	Shorts — White
Admitted to League: 1893	**Telephone No.:** (0709) 562434
Former Name(s): Thornhill United FC	**Ticket Information:** (0709) 562434
(1884-1905); Rotherham County FC (1905-	**Pitch Size:** 115 x 76yds
1925)	**Ground Capacity:** 14,000
Nickname: 'The Merry Millers'	**Seating Capacity:** 3,407
Ground: Millmoor Ground, Rotherham S60 1HR	

GENERAL INFORMATION
Supporters Club Administrator: Mrs. R. Cowley
Address: 50 Lister Street, Rotherham
Telephone Number: (0709) 375831
Car Parking: Kimberworth Road and Main Street Car Parks
Coach Parking: By Police Direction
Nearest Railway Station: Rotherham Central (½ mile)
Nearest Bus Station: Town Centre (½ mile)
Club Shop:
Opening Times: Mon-Sat 9.00-5.00
Telephone No.: (0709) 562760
Postal Sales: Yes
Nearest Police Station: Rotherham (½ mile)
Police Force: South Yorkshire
Police Telephone Number: (0709) 371121

GROUND INFORMATION
Away Supporters' Entrances: Millmoor Lane Turnstiles
Away Supporters' Sections: Millmoor Lane /Railway End
Family Facilities: Location of Stand: Millmoor Lane Side
Capacity of Stand: 748

DISABLED SUPPORTERS INFORMATION
Wheelchairs: Accommodated in Disabled Section, Millmoor Lane
Disabled Toilets: may be available 1991/92
The Blind: No Special Facilities

MILLMOOR LANE

MASBOROUGH STREET TIVOLI END

RAILWAY END (Away)

MAIN STAND

Travelling Supporters Information:
Routes: From North: Exit M1 junction 34 following Rotherham (A6109) signs to traffic lights and turn right into Millmoor Lane. Ground is ¼ mile on right over railway bridge. From South & West: Exit M1 junction 33, turn right following 'Rotherham' signs. Turn left at roundabout and right at next roundabout. Follow dual carriageway to next roundabout and go straight on. Turn left at next roundabout and ground is ¼ mile on left. From East: Take A630 into Rotherham following Sheffield signs. At 2nd roundabout turn right into Masborough Street then 1st left into Millmoor Lane.

SCARBOROUGH FC

Founded: 1879	**Record Attendance:** 11,124 (1938)
Turned Professional:	**Colours:** Shirts — Red
Limited Company: 1933	Shorts — White
Admitted to League: 1987	**Telephone No.:** (0723) 375094
Former Name(s): None	**Ticket Information:** (0723) 375094
Nickname: 'Boro'	**Pitch Size:** 112 x 74yds
Ground: McCain Stadium, Seamer Road	**Ground Capacity:** 10,000
Scarborough, N. Yorks	**Seating Capacity:** 864

GENERAL INFORMATION
Supporters Club Administrator: Dave Sidebottom
Address: 20 Almond Grove, Scarborough, North Yorkshire
Telephone Number: (0723) 371403
Car Parking: Street Parking
Coach Parking: At Ground
Nearest Railway Station: Scarborough Central (2 miles)
Nearest Bus Station: Westwood Scarborough (2 miles)
Club Shop:
Opening Times: Weekdays 9.30 5.00 & Satrudays 9.30-12.00 (Except Wednesday)
Telephone No.: (0723) 369211
Postal Sales: Yes
Nearest Police Station: Scarborough (2 miles)
Police Force: North Yorkshire
Police Telephone Number: (0723) 363333

GROUND INFORMATION
Away Supporters' Entrances: Edgehill Road turnstiles
Away Supporters' Sections: Visitors Enclosure, Edgehill Road End
Family Facilities: Location of Stand:
To right of Main Stand
Capacity of Stand: 200 standing

DISABLED SUPPORTERS INFORMATION
Wheelchairs: Accommodated
Disabled Toilets: None
The Blind: No Special Facilities

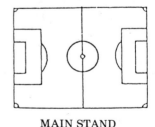

Travelling Supporters Information:
Routes: The Ground is situated on the main York to Scarborough Road (A64) ½ mile on left past B & Q DIY store.

SCUNTHORPE UNITED FC

Founded: 1899
Turned Professional: 1912
Limited Company: 1912
Admitted to League: 1950
Former Name(s): Scunthorpe and Lindsey United (1899/1912)
Nickname: 'Irons'
Ground: Glanford Park, Doncaster Road Scunthorpe, South Humberside DN15 8TD

Record Attendance: 8,775 (1/5/89)
Colours: Shirts — Sky Blue with Claret trim   Shorts — Sky Blue
Telephone No.: (0724) 848077
Ticket Information: (0724) 848077
Pitch Size: 111 x 73yds
Ground Capacity: 9,200
Seating Capacity: 6,400

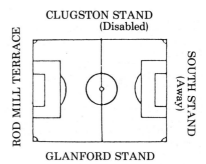

GENERAL INFORMATION
Supporters Club Administrator: Ian Burton
Address: 31 Goodwood, Bottesford, Scunthorpe.
Telephone Number: —
Car Parking: For 600 cars at Ground
Coach Parking: At Ground
Nearest Railway Station: Scunthorpe (1½ miles)
Nearest Bus Station: Scunthorpe (1½ miles)
Club Shop:
Opening Times: Weekdays and matchdays 9.00-5.00.
Telephone No.: (0724) 848077
Postal Sales: Yes
Nearest Police Station: Laneham Street, Scunthorpe (1½ miles)
Police Force: Humberside
Police Telephone Number: (0724) 843434

GROUND INFORMATION
Away Supporters' Entrances: Turnstiles 6-7
Away Supporters' Sections: South Stand
Family Facilities: Location of Stand: Clugston Stand
Capacity of Stand: 2,277
Away Families: Accommodated

DISABLED SUPPORTERS INFORMATION
Wheelchairs: Accommodated in Disabled Section (Clugston Stand)
Disabled Toilets: Yes
The Blind: Commentaries available

CLUGSTON STAND
(Disabled)

ROD MILL TERRACE

SOUTH STAND
(Away)

GLANFORD STAND

Travelling Supporters Information:
Routes: From All Parts: Exit M180 junction 3 on to M181. Follow M181 to roundabout with A18 and take A18 towards Scunthorpe — Ground on right

SHEFFIELD UNITED FC

Founded: 1889
Turned Professional: 1889
Limited Company: 1899
Admitted to League: 1892
Nickname: 'Blades
Ground: Bramall Lane, Sheffield S2 4SU

Record Attendance: 68,287 (15/2/36)
Colours: Shirts — Red & White Stripes
with black pinstripe   Shorts — Black
Telephone No.: (0742) 738955
Ticket Information: (0742) 738955
Pitch Size: 113 x 72yds
Ground Capacity: 35,606
Seating Capacity: 13,220

GENERAL INFORMATION
Supporters Club Administrator: Beryl Whitney
Address: 42 Base Green Ave., Sheffield S12 3FA
Telephone Number: (0742) 390202
Car Parking: Street Parking
Coach Parking: By Police Direction
Nearest Railway Station: Sheffield Midland (1 mile)
Nearest Bus Station: Pond Street, Sheffield
Club Shop:
Opening Times: Monday-Friday 9.30-5.00, Matchdays 9.30-5.30
Telephone No.: (0742) 750596
Postal Sales: Yes
Nearest Police Station: Police Room at Ground
Police Force: South Yorkshire
Police Telephone Number: (0742) 768522

GROUND INFORMATION
Away Supporters' Entrances: Bramall Lane Turnstiles
Away Supporters' Sections: Bramall Lane Stand & Terrace (Mostly covered)
Family Facilities: Location of Stand: New South Stand — West Wing
Capacity of Stand: 2,500 (Family section)
Away Families: Yes

DISABLED SUPPORTERS INFORMATION
Wheelchairs: Accommodated in Disabled Section — Members Area (Very limited space for visitors)
Disabled Toilets: Yes
The Blind: Commentaries on request

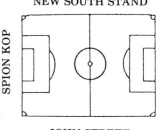

Travelling Supporters Information:
Routes: From North: Exit M1 junction 34 following signs to Sheffield (A6109), turn left 3½ miles and take 4th exit at roundabout into Sheaf Street. Take 5th exit at 2nd roundabout into St. Mary's Road (for Bakewell), turn left ½ mile into Bramall Lane; From South & East: Exit M1 junctions 31 or 33 and take A57 to roundabout, take 3rd exit into Sheaf Street (then as North); From West: Take A57 into Sheffield and take 4th exit at roundabout into Upper Hanover Street at 2nd roundabout take 3rd exit into Bramall Lane

SHEFFIELD WEDNESDAY FC

Founded: 1867	**Record Attendance:** 72,841 (17/2/34)
Turned Professional: 1887	**Colours:** Shirts — Blue & White Stripes
Limited Company: 1899	Shorts — Blue
Admitted to League: 1892	**Telephone No.:** (0742) 343122
Former Name(s): The Wednesday FC	**Ticket Information:** (0742) 337233
Nickname: 'Owls'	**Pitch Size:** 115 x 75yds
Ground: Hillsborough, Sheffield S6 1SW	**Ground Capacity:** 38,780
	Seating Capacity: 23,000

GENERAL INFORMATION
Supporters Club Administrator: Mrs Nettleship
Address: 260 Penistone Road, Sheffield
Telephone Number: (0742) 333419
Car Parking: Street Parking
Coach Parking: Owlerton Stadium
Nearest Railway Station: Sheffield Midland (4 miles)
Nearest Bus Station: Sheffield (4 miles)
Club Shop:
Opening Times: Monday-Saturday 10.00-4.30
Telephone No.: (0742) 343342
Postal Sales: Yes
Nearest Police Station: Hammerton Road Sheffield (1 mile)
Police Force: South Yorkshire
Police Telephone Number: (0742) 343131

GROUND INFORMATION
Away Supporters' Entrances: Leppings Lane Turnstiles
Away Supporters' Sections: West Stand
Family Facilities: Location of Stand: South Stand (uncovered section)
Capacity of Stand: 1,920
Away Families: None at present

DISABLED SUPPORTERS INFORMATION
Wheelchairs: Accommodated in Disabled Section (within North Stand)
Disabled Toilets: Yes
The Blind: Commentaries

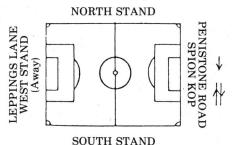

Travelling Supporters Information:
Routes: From North: Exit M1 junction 34 following signs to Sheffield (A6109), take 3rd exit (1½ miles) at roundabout and in 3¼ miles turn left into Herries Road South for ground; From South & East: Exit M1 junctions 31 or 33 and take A57 to roundabout, take exit into Prince of Wales Road after 5¾ miles turn left into Herries Road South; From West: Take A57 until A6101 and turn left. After 3¾ miles turn left at 'T' junction into Penistone Road for ground.

SHREWSBURY TOWN FC

Founded: 1886
Turned Professional: 1905
Limited Company: 1936
Admitted to League: 1950
Former Name(s): None
Nickname: 'Town' 'Shrews'
Ground: Gay Meadow, Shrewsbury, SY2 6AB

Record Attendance: 18,917 (26/4/61)
Colours: Shirts — Blue & Yellow Stripe
Shorts — White
Telephone No.: (0743) 360111
Ticket Information: (0743) 360111
Pitch Size: 116 x 75yds
Ground Capacity: 15,000
Seating Capacity: 4,500

GENERAL INFORMATION
Supporters Club Administrator: Fred Brown
Address: c/o Club
Telephone Number: (0743) 360111
Car Parking: Car Park Adjacent
Coach Parking: Gay Meadow
Nearest Railway Station: Shrewsbury (½ mile)
Nearest Bus Station: Baker Street, Shrewsbury
Club Shop:
Opening Times: Matchdays and Office Hours
Telephone No.: (0743) 356316
Postal Sales: Yes
Nearest Police Station: Clive Road Shrewsbury
Police Force: West Mercia
Police Telephone Number: (0743) 232888

GROUND INFORMATION

Away Supporters' Entrances: Station End Turnstiles
Away Supporters' Sections: Station Stand (covered)
Family Facilities: Location of Stand: Station Stand side
Capacity of Stand: 500
Away Families: By prior arrangement

DISABLED SUPPORTERS INFORMATION

Wheelchairs: Accommodated with difficulty (Please phone first — (0743) 360111)
Disabled Toilets: None
The Blind: No Special Facilities — but will help where possible

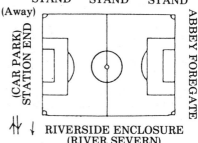

Travelling Supporters Information:

Routes: From North: Take A49 or A53 then 2nd exit at roundabout into Telford Way (A5112). After ¾ mile take 2nd exit at roundabout. Turn right at 'T' junction into Abbey Foregate for Ground. From South: Take A49 to Town Centre and at end of Coleham Head, turn right into Abbey Foregate; From East: Take A5 then A458 into Town Centre straight forward to Abbey Foregate; From West: Take A458 then A5 around Ring Road, Roman Road, then turn left into Hereford Road and at end of Coleman Head turn right into Abbey Foregate.

SOUTHAMPTON FC

Founded: 1885
Turned Professional: 1894
Limited Company: 1897
Admitted to League: 1920
Former Name(s): Southampton St. Marys
YMCA FC (1885/97)
Nickname: 'Saints'
Ground: The Dell, Milton Road,
Southampton, SO9 4XX

Record Attendance: 31,044 (8/10/69)
Colours: Shirts — Red and White
Shorts — Black
Telephone No.: (0703) 220505
Ticket Information: (0703) 228575
Pitch Size: 110 x 72yds
Ground Capacity: 21,989
Seating Capacity: 8,700

GENERAL INFORMATION
Supporters Club Administrator: The Secretary
Address: Saints Supporters' Social Club, The Dell, Milton Road, Southampton
Telephone Number: —
Car Parking: Street Parking
Coach Parking: By Police Direction
Nearest Railway Station: Southampton Central (1 mile)
Nearest Bus Station: West Quay Road, by Centre 2000
Club Shop:
Opening Times: Monday-Saturday 9.00-5.00
Telephone No.: (0703) 220505
Postal Sales: Yes
Nearest Police Station: Civic Centre, Southampton (1 mile)
Police Force: Hampshire
Police Telephone Number: (0703) 581111

GROUND INFORMATION
Away Supporters' Entrances: Archers Road Turnstiles
Away Supporters' Sections: Visitors enclosure Archers Road End (Open)
Family Facilities: Location of Stand: Elevated Terrace — Milton Road
Capacity of Stand: 2,876
Away Families: None

DISABLED SUPPORTERS INFORMATION
Wheelchairs: Limited Accommodation — Under West Stand
Disabled Toilets: Yes
The Blind: Commentaries available

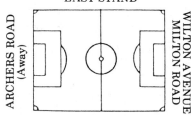

EAST STAND

ARCHERS ROAD
(Away)

WILTON AVENUE
MILTON ROAD

Blind   Wheelchairs
WEST STAND
HILL LANE/MILTON ROAD

Travelling Supporters Information:
Routes: From North: Take A33 into the Avenue and turn right into Northlands Road. Turn right at end into Archer's Road; From East: Take M27 to A334 and follow signs Southampton A3024. Then follow signs The West into Commercial Road, turn right into Hill Lane then 1st right into Milton Road; From West: Take A35 then A3024 following signs City Centre into Fourposts Hill then left into Hill Lane and 1st right into Milton Road

SOUTHEND UNITED FC

Founded: 1906
Turned Professional: 1906
Limited Company: 1919
Admitted to League: 1920
Former Name(s): Southend Athletic FC
Nickname: 'Shrimpers'/'Blues'
Ground: Roots Hall Ground, Victoria Avenue, Southend-on-Sea, SS2 6NQ

Record Attendance: 31,033 (10/1/79)
Colours: Shirts — Blue with Yellow trim
Shorts — Yellow
Telephone No.: (0702) 340707
Ticket Information: (0839) 664443
Pitch Size: 110 x 74yds
Ground Capacity: 15,000
Seating Capacity: 4,250

GENERAL INFORMATION
Supporters Club Administrator:
B. Harris
Address: c/o Club
Telephone Number: (0702) 342707
Car Parking: Car Park at Ground (500 cars) — Season Ticket Holders Only
Coach Parking: Car Park
Nearest Railway Station: Prittlewell (½ mile)
Nearest Bus Station: London Road, Southend
Club Shop:
Opening Times: Weekdays & Matchdays 10.30-4.30 p.m. (except Wednesday)
Telephone No.: (0702) 345067
Postal Sales: Yes
Nearest Police Station: Southend-on-Sea (¼ mile)
Police Force: Essex
Police Telephone Number: (0702) 431212

GROUND INFORMATION
Away Supporters' Entrances: East Stand-turnstiles
Away Supporters' Sections: South Bank Terrace (Open)
Family Facilities: Location of Stand: East Stand
Capacity of Stand: 2,840

DISABLED SUPPORTERS INFORMATION
Wheelchairs: Accommodated in Disabled Section — West Stand
Disabled Toilets: Yes
The Blind: Commentaries

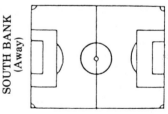

SHAKESPEARE DRIVE
WEST STAND
SOUTH BANK (Away)
FAIRFAX DRIVE NORTH BANK
EAST STAND
VICTORIA AVENUE

Travelling Supporters Information:
Routes: From North & West: Take A127 into Southend then at roundabout take 3rd exit into Victoria Avenue; From South: Take A13 following signs for Southend and turn left into West Road. At the end of West Road turn left into Victoria Avenue.

STOCKPORT COUNTY FC

Founded: 1883	**Record Attendance:** 27,833 (11/2/50)
Turned Professional: 1891	**Colours:** Shirts — Blue
Limited Company: 1908	Shorts — Blue
Admitted to League: 1900	**Telephone No.:** (061) 480 8888
Former Name(s): Heaton Norris Rovers	**Ticket Information:** (061) 480 8888
FC; Heaton Norris FC	**Pitch Size:** 111 x 71yds
Nickname: 'Hatters' 'County'	**Ground Capacity:** 8,500
Ground: Edgeley Park, Hardcastle Road,	**Seating Capacity:** 1,800
Edgeley, Stockport SK3 9DD	

GENERAL INFORMATION
Supporters Club Administrator: K. Boxshall
Address: c/o Club
Telephone Number: —
Car Parking: Street Parking
Coach Parking: By Police Direction
Nearest Railway Station: Stockport (5 minutes walk)
Nearest Bus Station: Mersey Square (10 minutes walk)
Club Shop:
Opening Times: Weekdays & match days 9.00-5.00 p.m.
Telephone No.: (061) 480 1247
Postal Sales: Yes
Nearest Police Station: Stockport (1 mile)
Police Force: Greater Manchester
Police Telephone Number: (061) 872 5050

GROUND INFORMATION
Away Supporters' Entrances: Railway End Turnstiles
Away Supporters' Sections: Railway End
Family Facilities: Location of Stand: In front of Main Stand
Capacity of Stand: 1,800
Away Families: No

DISABLED SUPPORTERS INFORMATION
Wheelchairs: Accommodated at front of Main Stand
Disabled Toilets: None
The Blind: No Special Facilities

Travelling Supporters Information:
Routes: From North, South & West: Exit M63 junction 11 and join A560, following signs for Cheadle, after ¼ mile turn right into Edgeley Road and in 1 mile turn right into Caroline Street for ground; From East: Take A6 or A560 into Stockport Town Centre and turn left into Greek Street. Take 2nd exit into Mercian Way (from roundabout) then turn left into Caroline Street — ground straight ahead.

STOKE CITY FC

Founded: 1863
Turned Professional: 1885
Limited Company: 1908
Admitted to League: 1888 (Founder)
Former Name(s): Stoke FC
Nickname: 'Potters'
Ground: Victoria Ground, Boothen Old Road, Stoke-On-Trent ST4 4EG

Record Attendance: 51,380 (29/3/37)
Colours: Shirts — Red & White Stripes
Shorts — White
Telephone No.: (0782) 413511
Ticket Information: (0782) 413961
Pitch Size: 116 x 72 yds
Ground Capacity: 25,084
Seating Capacity: 9,625

GENERAL INFORMATION
Supporters Club Administrator: Nic Mansfield
Address: 11A Westland Street, Penkhull, Stoke-on-Trent ST4 7HE
Telephone Number: (0782) 48000
Car Parking: Car Park at Ground (2,000 cars)
Coach Parking: Whieldon Road
Nearest Railway Station: Stoke-on-Trent (10 minutes walk)
Nearest Bus Station: Hanley (2 miles)
Club Shop:
Opening Times: Monday to Friday 9.30-5.00 & Saturdays 9.30-12.00
Telephone No.: (0782) 747047
Postal Sales: Yes
Nearest Police Station: Stoke-On-Trent (¼ mile)
Police Force: Staffordshire
Police Telephone Number: (0782) 744644

GROUND INFORMATION
Away Supporters' Entrances: Butler Street Turnstiles
Away Supporters' Sections: Butler Street Stand & Stoke End Paddock
Family Facilities: Location of Stand: Stoke End Stand
Capacity of Stand: 2,000
Away Families: None

DISABLED SUPPORTERS INFORMATION
Wheelchairs: Accommodated in Disabled Section (by prior arrangement) — Corner Butler Street / Boothen End
Disabled Toilets: None
The Blind: Limited Facilities — Phone First

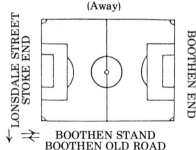

Travelling Supporters Information:
Routes: From North, South & West: Exit M6 junction 15 and follow signs Stoke (A5006) and join A500 Branch left ¾ mile and take 2nd exit at roundabout into Campbell Road for Ground; From East: Take A50 into Stoke Town Centre and turn left at crossroads into Lonsdale Street for Campbell Road.

SUNDERLAND AFC

Founded: 1879	**Record Attendance:** 75,118 (8/3/33)
Turned Professional: 1886	**Colours:** Shirts — Red and White stripes
Limited Company: 1906	Shorts — Black
Admitted to League: 1890	**Telephone No.:** (091) 514 0332
Former Name(s): Sunderland & District	**Ticket Information:** (091) 514 0332
Teachers FC	**Pitch Size:** 113 x 74yds
Nickname: 'Rokerites'	**Ground Capacity:** 31,887
Ground: Roker Park, Grantham Road,	**Seating Capacity:** 8,989
Roker, Sunderland, SR6 9SW	

GENERAL INFORMATION
Supporters Club Administrator: Audrey Baillie
Address: 36 Roker Baths Road, Roker, Sunderland
Telephone Number: (091) 567 0067
Car Parking: Car Park for 1,500 cars
Coach Parking: Seafront, Roker
Nearest Railway Station: Seaburn
Nearest Bus Station: Town Centre (2 miles)
Club Shop: Town Centre & Roker Park
Opening Times: Monday-Saturday 9.00-5.00.
Telephone No.: (091) 567 2336
Postal Sales: Yes
Nearest Police Station: Wheatsheaf (½ mile)
Police Force: Northumbria
Police Telephone Number: (091) 567 6155

GROUND INFORMATION
Away Supporters' Entrances: Roker End turnstiles
Away Supporters' Sections: Roker End
Family Facilities: Location of Stand: Centre Stand
Capacity of Stand: 1,200
Away Families: Yes

DISABLED SUPPORTERS INFORMATION
Wheelchairs: Accommodated in Disabled Section — Roker End
Disabled Toilets: Yes
The Blind: Headphone Commentaries in Disabled Section

Travelling Supporters Information:
Routes: From North: Take A184 — Sunderland. Through Boldon ¼ mile after Greyhound Stadium at roundabout, straight on for Town Centre (A1018). Left at "T" junction. At traffic lights (Blue Bell Pub) turn right. Follow road for ¾ mile and turn left, sign posted for Roker Park; From South: A19 or A1M take turn-off for A1231 Sunderland North. A1M—A690 Sunderland, left onto A19 towards Tyne Tunnel & Gateshead. Take A1231 Sunderland North, then follow signs for Town Centre. After 2 miles at traffic lights, straight ahead in left lane marked A1289 Roker. After 1 mile follow Roker A183 signs. After 200 yards follow signs for Whitburn & Sea Front (A183). After ½ mile turn left down side street, the Football Ground is straight ahead.

SWANSEA CITY FC

Founded: 1900	**Record Attendance:** 32,796 (17/2/68)
Turned Professional: 1912	**Colours:** Shirts — White
Limited Company: 1912	Shorts — White
Admitted to League: 1920	**Telephone No.:** (0792) 474114
Former Name(s): Swansea Town FC	**Ticket Information:** (0792) 474114
(1900/70)	**Pitch Size:** 110 x 74 yds
Nickname: 'Swans'	**Ground Capacity:** 16,419
Ground: Vetch Field, Swansea SA1 3SU	**Seating Capacity:** 3,414

GENERAL INFORMATION
Supporters Club Administrator: John Button
Address: 159 Western St., Swansea
Telephone Number: (0792) 460958
Car Parking: Kingsway Car Park (200 yards)
Coach Parking: By Police Direction
Nearest Railway Station: Swansea High Street (½ mile)
Nearest Bus Station: Quadrant Depot (¼ mile)
Club Shop: 33 William St., Swansea SA1 3QS
Opening Times: Weekdays 9.30-4.30, Matchdays 9.30-5.00
Telephone No.: (0792) 462584
Postal Sales: Yes
Nearest Police Station: Swansea Central (½ mile)
Police Force: South Wales
Police Telephone Number: (0792) 456999

GROUND INFORMATION
Away Supporters' Entrances: Richardson Street turnstiles
Away Supporters' Sections: West Terrace Enclosure (part covered)
Family Facilities: Location of Stand: Jewson Family Enclosure (West Side of Centre Stand)
Capacity of Stand: 321 seats
Away Families: None

DISABLED SUPPORTERS INFORMATION
Wheelchairs: Accommodated — Centre Stand Touchline
Disabled Toilets: None
The Blind: No Special Facilities

Travelling Supporters Information:
Routes: From All Parts: Exit M4 junction 45 and follow Swansea (A4067) signs into City Centre along High Street. Passing Railway Station into Castle Station then Wind Street and take 3rd exit at roundabout into Victoria Road and bear right towards bus station at Quadrant for Ground.

SWINDON TOWN FC

Founded: 1881
Turned Professional: 1895
Limited Company: 1897
Admitted to League: 1920
Former Name(s): None
Nickname: 'Robins'
Ground: County Ground, County Road, Swindon, SN1 2ED

Record Attendance: 32,000 (15/1/72)
Colours: Shirts — Red
Shorts — White
Telephone No.: (0793) 430430
Ticket Information: (0793) 430430
Pitch Size: 114 x 72 yds
Ground Capacity: 16,432
Seating Capacity: 7,500

GENERAL INFORMATION
Supporters Club Administrator: Miss S. Cobern
Address: 12 Deburgh Street, Rodbourne, Swindon
Telephone Number: (0793) 481061
Car Parking: Car Park adjacent
Coach Parking: Car Park adjacent
Nearest Railway Station: Swindon (½ mile)
Nearest Bus Station: Swindon (½ mile)
Club Shop: Robins Corner
Opening Times: Weekdays 9.00-6.00, (closes 12.00-2.00) Saturdays 9.00-1.00 (or kick-off on Matchdays)
Telephone No.: (0793) 642984 ext. 29
Postal Sales: Yes
Nearest Police Station: Fleming Way, Swindon
Police Force: Wiltshire
Police Telephone Number: (0793) 528111

GROUND INFORMATION
Away Supporters' Entrances: Visitors Enclosure turnstiles — Stratton Bank
Away Supporters' Sections: Visitors Enclosure Stratton Bank (open)
Family Facilities: Location of Stand: Town End Stand
Capacity of Stand: 500
Away Families: None

DISABLED SUPPORTERS INFORMATION
Wheelchairs: Accommodated in Disabled Section — in North Stand
Disabled Toilets: None
The Blind: Commentaries in Disabled Section

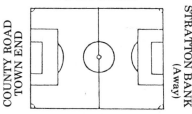

NORTH STAND

COUNTY ROAD
TOWN END

STRATTON BANK (Away)

SOUTH STAND
SHRIVENHAM ROAD

Travelling Supporters Information:
Routes: From London & East and South: Exit M4 junction 15 and take A345 into Swindon along Queen's Drive, take 3rd exit at 'Magic Roundabout' into County Road. From West: Exit M4 junction 16 and take A420 into Swindon and take 1st exit at roundabout into Westcott Place and follow into Faringdon Road to Fleet Street, Milford Street and Manchester Road. Exit right at roundabout into County Road. From North: Take M4 or A345/A420/A361 to County Road roundabout then as above.

TORQUAY UNITED FC

Founded: 1898
Turned Professional: 1921
Limited Company: 1921
Admitted to League: 1927
Former Name(s): Torquay Town
(1898-1910)
Nickname: 'Gulls'
Ground: Plainmoor Ground, Torquay
TQ1 3PS

Record Attendance: 21,908 (29/1/55)
Colours: Shirts — Yellow & White Stripe/
Navy Trim   Shorts — Navy
Telephone No.: (0803) 328666/7
Ticket Information: (0803) 328666/7
Pitch Size: 112 x 74yds
Ground Capacity: 5,639
Seating Capacity: 1,476
Fax No: (0803) 323976

GENERAL INFORMATION
Supporters Club Administrator: Mrs.
A. Smith
Address: 1 Cedar Court Road, Torquay
Telephone Number: (0803) 313510
Car Parking: Street Parking
Coach Parking: Lymington Road
Coach Station (½ mile)
Nearest Railway Station: Torquay (2
miles)
Nearest Bus Station: Lymington Road
(½ mile)
Club Shop:
Opening Times: Matchdays and during
office hours
Telephone No.: (0803) 328666
Postal Sales: Yes
Nearest Police Station: Torquay (1
mile)
Police Force: Devon & Cornwall
Police Telephone Number: (0803)
214491

GROUND INFORMATION
Away Supporters' Entrances: Babbacombe
End Turnstiles
Away Supporters' Sections: Babbacombe End
Family Facilities: Location of Stand:
Ellacombe End — Torcroft Family Stand
Capacity of Stand: 500 (Family Part)

DISABLED SUPPORTERS INFORMATION
Wheelchairs: Accommodated by prior arrangement
Disabled Toilets: Yes
The Blind: Audio Facilities

(MAIN STAND)
HOMELANDS LANE

WARBRO ROAD
BABBACOMBE END
(Away)

ELLACOMBE END
TORCROFT FAMILY STAND

MARNHAM ROAD
POPULAR SIDE

Travelling Supporters Information:
Routes: From North & East: Take M5 to A38 and A380 to Kingskerwell. Take 1st exit at roundabout (1 mile) and in 1 mile turn left following Babbacombe (A3022) signs. Turn left (¾ mile) into Westhill road for Warbro Road. From West: Take A380 into Town Centre and follow signs Teignmouth (A379) to Lymington Road. Turn right into Upton Hill and follow into Bronshill Road. Take 2nd left into Derwent Road and at end turn right and right again into Marnham Road.

TOTTENHAM HOTSPUR FC

Founded: 1882
Turned Professional: 1895
Limited Company: 1898
Admitted to League: 1908
Former Name(s): Hotspur FC (1882/5)
Nickname: 'Spurs'
Ground: White Hart Lane, 748 High Road Tottenham, London N17 OAP

Record Attendance: 75,038 (5/3/38)
Colours: Shirts — White
    Shorts — Navy Blue
Telephone No.: (081) 808 8080
Ticket Information: (081) 808 1020
Pitch Size: 110 x 73yds
Ground Capacity: 34,797
Seating Capacity: 16,266

GENERAL INFORMATION
Supporters Club Administrator: Chris Belt
Address: Spurs Members Club, 748 High Road.
Telephone Number: (081) 808 8080
Car Parking: None within ¼ mile
Coach Parking: Northumberland Park Coach Park
Nearest Railway Station: White Hart Lane (nearby)
Nearest Tube Station: Seven Sisters (Victoria) Manor House (Piccadilly)
Club Shop:
Opening Times: Weekdays 9.30-5.30 and Matchdays 9.30-6.00
Telephone No.: (081) 801 1669
Postal Sales: Yes
Nearest Police Station: Tottenham (1 mile)
Police Force: Metropolitan
Police Telephone Number: (081) 801 3443

GROUND INFORMATION
Away Supporters' Entrances: Park Lane, Turn-stiles 56-59 (seats), 60-65 & 76-79 (standing)
Away Supporters' Sections: South Stand, Park Lane
Family Facilities: Location of Stand: Members Stand
Capacity of Stand: 4,305 Standing, 3,405 Seats
Away Families: None

DISABLED SUPPORTERS INFORMATION
Wheelchairs: Accommodated by prior arrangement — Paxton Road End
Disabled Toilets: Yes
The Blind: No Special Facilities

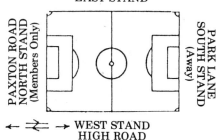

Travelling Supporters Information:
Routes: From All Parts: Take A406 North Circular to Edmonton and at traffic lights follow signs for Tottenham (A1010) into Fore Street for Ground.

TRANMERE ROVERS FC

Founded: 1881
Turned Professional: 1912
Limited Company: 1920
Admitted to League: 1921
Former Name(s): Belmont FC
Nickname: 'Rovers'
Ground: Prenton Park, Prenton Road West, Birkenhead L42 9PN

Record Attendance: 24,424 (5/2/72)
Colours: Shirts — White
Shorts — White
Telephone No.: (051) 608 3677
Pitch Size: 112 x 74yds
Ground Capacity: 14,200
Seating Capacity: 3,800

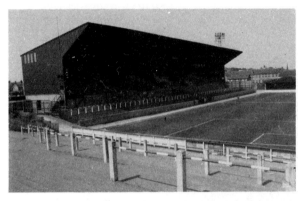

GENERAL INFORMATION
Supporters Club Administrator: Martin Decker
Address: c/o Club
Telephone Number: (051) 608 3677
Car Parking: Large Car Park at Ground
Coach Parking: At Ground
Nearest Railway Station: Hamilton Square, Rock Ferry (1 mile)
Nearest Bus Station: Birkenhead
Club Shop:
Opening Times: Weekdays and matchdays 9.00-5.00
Telephone No.: (051) 608 0438
Postal Sales: Yes
Nearest Police Station: Bebington (2 miles)
Police Force: Merseyside
Police Telephone Number: (051) 709 6010

GROUND INFORMATION
Away Supporters' Entrances: Bebington End turnstiles — access from main car park
Away Supporters' Sections: Bebington End (open)
Family Facilities: Location of Stand: Family Enclosure
Capacity of Stand: 3,800
Away Families: Yes

DISABLED SUPPORTERS INFORMATION
Wheelchairs: Accommodated in Disabled Section (Family enclosure)
Disabled Toilets: Two available
The Blind: No Special Facilities

CAR PARK
FAMILY ENCLOSURE   MAIN STAND

BEBINGTON KOP END (Away)

PRENTON ROAD WEST

TOWN END

BOROUGH ROAD SIDE

Travelling Supporters Information:
Routes: From North: Take Mersey Tunnel to M53, exit junction 3 and take 1st exit at roundabout (A552), in 1¼ mile turn right at crossroads (B5151) then left into Prenton Road West; From South and East: Exit M53 junction 4 and take 4th exit at roundabout (B5151). After 2½ miles turn right into Prenton Road West.

WALSALL FC

Founded: 1888	**Record Attendance:** 10,628 (20/5/91
Turned Professional: 1888	England B v Switzerland)
Limited Company: 1921	**Colours:** Shirts — Red
Admitted to League: 1892	Shorts — White
Former Name(s): Walsall Town Swifts FC	**Telephone No.:** (0922) 22791
(1888/95)	**Ticket Information:** (0922) 22791
Nickname: 'Saddlers'	**Pitch Size:** 110 x 73yds
Ground: Bescot Stadium, Bescot Crescent	**Ground Capacity:** 10,400
Walsall, West Midlands WS1 4SA	**Seating Capacity:** 4,500

GENERAL INFORMATION

Supporters Club Administrator: John Wilson
Address: Saddlers Club, Wallows Lane, Walsall
Telephone Number: (0922) 22257
Car Parking: Car Park at Ground
Coach Parking: At Ground
Nearest Railway Station: Bescot (adjacent)
Nearest Bus Station: Bradford Place
Club Shop:
Opening Times: Weekdays & Matchdays 9.00-4.30 p.m.
Telephone No.: (0922) 22791
Postal Sales: Yes
Nearest Police Station: Walsall (2 miles)
Police Force: West Midlands
Police Telephone Number: (0922) 38111

GROUND INFORMATION

Away Supporters' Entrances: William Sharp Stand Turnstiles
Away Supporters' Sections: Highgate Mild Stand (Seating), William Sharp Stand (Standing)
Family Facilities: Location of Stand: In front of Highgate Mild Stand — Blocks A & B
Capacity of Stand: — 448 seats
Away Families: Yes

DISABLED SUPPORTERS INFORMATION

Wheelchairs: Accommodated in Highgate Mild Stand
Disabled Toilets: Yes
The Blind: Commentaries planned

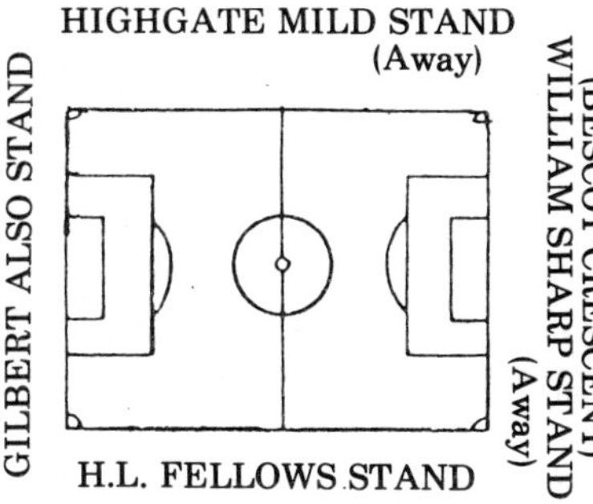

HIGHGATE MILD STAND
(Away)

GILBERT ALSO STAND

(BESCOT CRESCENT)
WILLIAM SHARP STAND
(Away)

H.L. FELLOWS STAND

Travelling Supporters Information:

Routes: From All Parts: Exit M6 junction 9 turning North towards Walsall on to the A461. After ¼ mile turn right into Wallows Lane and pass over railway bridge. Then take 1st right into Bescot Crescent and ground is ½ mile along on left adjacent to Bescot Railway Station.

WATFORD FC

Founded: 1891	**Record Attendance:** 34,099 (3/2/69)
Turned Professional: 1897	**Colours:** Shirts — Yellow with Black & Red Band
Limited Company: 1909	
Admitted to League: 1920	Shorts — Red with Yellow & Black Trim
Former Name(s): Formed by Amalgamation of West Herts FC & St. Marys FC	**Telephone No:** (0923) 30933
	Ticket Information: (0923) 220393
Nickname: 'Hornets'	**Pitch Size:** 115 x 75yds
Ground: Vicarage Road Stadium, Watford WD1 8ER	**Ground Capacity:** 23,596
	Seating Capacity: 6,906

GENERAL INFORMATION
Supporters Club Administrator: Mike Sullivan
Address: c/o Club
Telephone Number: (0923) 30933
Car Parking: Nearby Multi-Storey Car Parks
Coach Parking: Cardiff Road Car Park
Nearest Railway Station: Station at Ground (for big games)
Nearest Bus Station: Watford
Club Shop:
Opening Times: Tuesday-Saturday 9.00-5.00
Telephone No.: (0923) 220847
Postal Sales: Yes
Nearest Police Station: Shady Lane, Clarendon Road, Watford (1½ miles)
Police Force: Hertfordshire
Police Telephone Number: (0923) 244444

GROUND INFORMATION
Away Supporters' Entrances: Entrance Z
Away Supporters' Sections: South West Terrace (Part covered)
Family Facilities: Location of Stand: East Stand
Capacity of Stand: 750 seated in Family Block, 1,250 in Family Terrace
Away Families: Subject to Availability of Tickets (phone first)

DISABLED SUPPORTERS INFORMATION
Wheelchairs: Accommodated in Disabled Section (East Stand)
Disabled Toilets: Yes
The Blind: Commentaries in Disabled Section (East Stand)

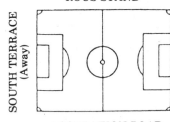

Travelling Supporters Information:
Routes: From North: Exit M1 junction 6 following signs for Watford A405/A41 & A411. Follow signs Slough A412 and turn left (¾ mile) into Harwoods Road. Turn left at 'T' junction into Vicarage Road; From South & East: Exit M1 junction 5 and follow signs to Watford (A41) & A412. Follow signs for Slough (then as North); From West: Take A412 past Croxley Green Station and turn right (1 mile) into Harwoods Road (then as North).

WEST BROMWICH ALBION FC

Founded: 1879
Turned Professional: 1885
Limited Company: 1892
Admitted to League: 1888 (Founder)
Former Name(s): West Bromwich Strollers (1879-1880)
Nickname: 'Throstles' 'Baggies' 'Albion'
Ground: The Hawthorns, Halfords Lane, West Bromwich, West Midlands B71 4LF

Record Attendance: 64,815 (6/3/37)
Colours: Shirts — Navy Blue and White Stripes.
Shorts — Navy Blue
Telephone No.: (021) 525 8888
Ticket Information: (021) 553 5472
Pitch Size: 115 x 75yds
Ground Capacity: 31,700
Seating Capacity: 12,550

GENERAL INFORMATION
Supporters Club Administrator: David Knott
Address: c/o 44 Hollyhedge Road, West Bromwich, West Midlands B71 3AB
Telephone Number: (021) 588 6549
Car Parking: Halfords Lane Car Parks, Rainbow Stand Car Park
Coach Parking: Rainbow Stand Car Park
Nearest Railway Station: Rolfe Street, Smethwick (1½ miles)
Nearest Bus Station: Town Centre
Club Shop:
Opening Times: Weekdays 9.00-5.00; Matchdays 9.00-2.45
Telephone No.: (021) 525 8888
Postal Sales: Yes
Nearest Police Station: Holyhead Road, Handsworth (½ mile)
Police Force: West Midlands
Police Telephone Number: (021) 554 3414

GROUND INFORMATION
Away Supporters' Entrances: Smethwick End turnstiles (P-Block)
Away Supporters' Sections: Smethwick End (covered)
Family Facilities: Location of Stand: Halfords Lane Stand (M Block)
Capacity of Stand: 500

DISABLED SUPPORTERS INFORMATION
Wheelchairs: Accommodated — Corner Birmingham Road End/Main Stand
Disabled Toilets: Yes
The Blind: No Special Facilities

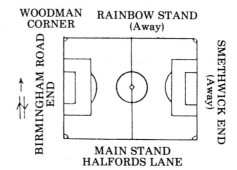

Travelling Supporters Information:
Routes: From All Parts: Exit M5 junction 1 and take Birmingham Road (A41) for ground.

WEST HAM UNITED FC

Founded: 1895	**Record Attendance:** 42,322 (17/10/70)
Turned Professional: 1900	**Colours:** Shirts — Claret & Blue
Limited Company: 1900	Shorts — White
Admitted to League: 1919	**Telephone No.:** (081) 472 2740
Former Name(s): None	**Ticket Information:** (081) 472 3322
Nickname: 'Hammers'	**Pitch Size:** 112 x 72yds
Ground: Boleyn Ground, Green Street	**Ground Capacity:** 28,863
Upton Park, London E13 9AZ	**Seating Capacity:** 11,600

GENERAL INFORMATION
Supporters Club Administrator: Mr. T. Jenkinson
Address: West Ham Supporters' Club, Castle Street, East Ham, E6
Telephone Number: (081) 472 1680
Car Parking: Street Parking
Coach Parking: By Police Direction
Nearest Railway Station: Upton Park (5 minutes walk)
Nearest Tube Station: Upton Park (5 minutes walk)
Club Shop: The Hammers Shop
Opening Times: Weekdays & Matchdays 9.30-5.30
Telephone No.: (081) 472 4214
Postal Sales: Yes
Nearest Police Station: East Ham High Street South (½ mile)
Police Force: Metropolitan
Police Telephone Number: (081) 593 8232

GROUND INFORMATION
Away Supporters' Entrances: Turnstiles 23-29, Castle Street
Away Supporters' Sections: South Bank West Side (Part Covered)
Family Facilities: Location of Stand: East Stand Side
Capacity of Stand: 905
Away Families: None

DISABLED SUPPORTERS INFORMATION
Wheelchairs: Limited Accommodation in disabled area (telephone in advance)
Disabled Toilets: Yes
The Blind: No Special Facilities

PRIORY ROAD
EAST STAND
NORTH BANK
CASTLE STREET
SOUTH BANK
(Away)
WEST STAND
GREEN STREET

Travelling Supporters Information:
Routes: From North & West: Take North Circular (A406), to A124 (East Ham) then on Barking Road for approximately 1½ miles until approaching traffic lights at crossroads. Turn right into Green Street, ground is on right-hand side; From South: Take Blackwall Tunnel and A13 to Canning Town. Follow signs for East Ham (A124). After 1¾ miles turn left into Green Street; From East: Take A13 and turn right on to A117 at crossroads. After approximately 1 mile turn left at crossroads onto A124. Turn right (¾ mile) into Green Street.

WIGAN ATHLETIC FC

Founded: 1932	**Record Attendance:** 27,500 (12/12/51)
Turned Professional: 1932	**Colours:** Shirts — Blue
Limited Company: 1932	Shorts — White
Admitted to League: 1978	**Telephone No.:** (0942) 44433
Former Name(s): None	**Ticket Information:** (0942) 44433
Nickname: 'Latics'	**Pitch Size:** 117 x 73yds
Ground: Springfield Park, Wigan	**Ground Capacity:** 12,500
Lancs. WN6 7BA	**Seating Capacity:** 1,272

GENERAL INFORMATION
Supporters Club Administrator:
Stuart Cooper
Address: c/o Club
Telephone Number: (0942) 43512
Car Parking: Street Parking only
Coach Parking: Shevington End
Nearest Railway Station: Wallgate &
North West (1 mile)
Nearest Bus Station: Wigan
Club Shop:
Opening Times: Weekdays & Matchdays 9.00-5.00
Telephone No.: (0942) 44433
Postal Sales: Yes
Nearest Police Station: Harrogate
Street, Wigan (1 mile)
Police Force: Greater Manchester
Police Telephone Number: (0942)
44981

GROUND INFORMATION
Away Supporters' Entrances: Shevington End
Turnstiles
Away Supporters' Sections: Shevington End
(Part Covered)
Family Facilities: Location of Stand:
In front of Phoenix Stand (Heinz Family
Enclosure)
Capacity of Stand: 128
Away Families: By prior arrangement

DISABLED SUPPORTERS INFORMATION
Wheelchairs: Accommodated — (Phoenix
Stand)
Disabled Toilets: None
The Blind: Commentaries — Phoenix Stand

Travelling Supporters Information:
Routes: From North: Exit M6 junction 27 following signs for Wigan (A5209), turn right (¼ mile) (B5206). Turn left 1 mile and in 4½ miles take left into Springfield Road. From South: Exit M6 junction 25 following signs for Wigan (A49). Turn left into Robin Park Road and into Scot Lane. Turn right at 3rd traffic lights into Woodhouse Lane and left at traffic lights into Springfield Road. From East: Take A557 into Town Centre then left into Robin Park Road (then as South)

WIMBLEDON FC

Founded: 1889	**Record Attendance:** 51,482 (11/5/79)
Turned Professional: 1964	**Colours:** Shirts — Blue
Limited Company: 1964	Shorts — Blue
Admitted to League: 1977	**Telephone No.:** (081) 653 4462
Former Name(s): Wimbledon Old Centrals	**Ticket Information:** (081) 653 4462
FC (1889/1905)	**Pitch Size:** 110 x 75yds
Nickname: 'Dons'	**Ground Capacity:** 29,949
Ground: Selhurst Park, London	**Seating Capacity:** 15,135
SE25 6PU	

GENERAL INFORMATION
Supporters Club Administrator:
Sandra Lowne
Address: c/o Club
Telephone Number: (081) 653 4462
Car Parking: Street Parking
Coach Parking: Thornton Heath
Nearest Railway Station: Selhurst /Norwood Junction/Thornton Heath
Nearest Bus Station: Norwood Junction
Club Shop:
Opening Times: Weekdays & Matchdays 9.30-5.30
Telephone No.: (081) 653 5584
Postal Sales: Yes
Nearest Police Station: South Norwood (15 minutes walk)
Police Force: Metropolitan
Police Telephone Number: (081) 653 8568

GROUND INFORMATION
Away Supporters' Entrances: Park Road/ Holmesdale Road
Away Supporters' Sections: Corner — Park Road & Holmesdale Road (Open Terrace & Covered Seating)
Family Facilities: Location of Stand: Members Stand (Clifton Road End)
Capacity of Stand: 4,600

DISABLED SUPPORTERS INFORMATION
Wheelchairs: Accommodated, Disabled Section in Arthur Wait Stand. (Park Road Entrance, free of charge)
Disabled Toilets: Yes in Crystals Banquet Suite
The Blind: Commentaries

PARK ROAD
ARTHUR WAIT STAND
ARTHUR WAIT ENCLOSURE

WHITEHORSE LANE
MEMBERS TERRACE

HOLMESDALE ROAD (Away)

MEMBERS STAND
CLIFTON ROAD

Travelling Supporters Information:
Routes: From North: Take M1/A1 to North Circular (A406) to Chiswick. Take South Circular (A205) to Wandsworth, take A3 to A214 and follow signs to Streatham to A23. Turn left onto B273 (1 mile), follow to end and turn left into High Street and into Whitehorse Lane; From East: Take A232 (Croydon Road) to Shirley and join A215 (Norwood Road), after 2¼ miles take left into Whitehorse Lane; From South: Take A23 and follow signs Crystal Palace B266 through Thornton Heath into Whitehorse Lane; From West: Take M4 to Chiswick (then as North).

WOLVERHAMPTON WANDERERS FC

Founded: 1877
Turned Professional: 1888
Limited Company: 1892
Admitted to League: 1888 (Founder)
Former Name(s): St. Lukes FC & The Wanderers FC (Combined 1880)
Nickname: 'Wolves'
Ground: Molineux Ground, Waterloo Road, Wolverhampton WV1 4QR

Record Attendance: 61,315 (11/2/39)
Colours: Shirts — Gold
Shorts — Black
Telephone No.: (0902) 712181
Ticket Information: (0902) 25899
Pitch Size: 116 x 74yds
Ground Capacity: 25,000
Seating Capacity: 9,500

GENERAL INFORMATION
Supporters Club Administrator: Albert Bates
Address: 341 Penn Road, Penn, Wolverhampton
Telephone Number: (0902) 330322
Car Parking: Around West Park & Rear of North Bank
Coach Parking: By Police Direction
Nearest Railway Station: Wolverhampton (1 mile)
Nearest Bus Station: Wolverhampton (1 mile)
Club Shop:
Opening Times: Weekdays & Matchdays 9.00-5.00
Telephone No.: (0902) 27524
Postal Sales: Yes
Nearest Police Station: Dunstall Road (500 yards)
Police Force: West Midlands
Police Telephone Number: (0902) 27851

GROUND INFORMATION
Away Supporters' Entrances: South Bank turnstiles
Away Supporters' Sections: South Bank (part covered)
Family Facilities: Location of Stand: John Ireland Lower Tier
Capacity of Stand: —

DISABLED SUPPORTERS INFORMATION
Wheelchairs: Accommodated in Disabled Section — Corner of John Ireland Stand
Disabled Toilets: Yes
The Blind: No Special Facilities

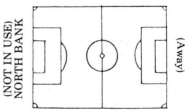

MOLINEUX STREET
JOHN IRELAND STAND

(NOT IN USE) NORTH BANK

SOUTH BANK (Away)

(NOT IN USE)
WATERLOO ROAD STAND

Travelling Supporters Information:
Routes: From North: Exit M6 junction 12 following signs for Wolverhampton A5, then A449 and at roundabout take 2nd exit into Waterloo Road then turn left into Molyneux Street; From South: Exit M5 junction 2 following signs for Wolverhampton A4123, turn right, then left into Ring Road, turn left (1 mile) into Waterloo Road, then turn right into Molineux Street; From East: Exit M6 junction 10 following signs Wolverhampton A454, turn right at crossroads into Stratford Street then turn left (¼ mile) into Ring Road, right at crossroads into Waterloo Road then right into Molineux Street; From West: Take A454 and at roundabout turn left into Ring Road (then as East).

WREXHAM FC

Founded: 1873	**Record Attendance:** 34,445 (26/1/57)
Turned Professional: 1912	**Colours:** Shirts — Red
Limited Company: 1912	Shorts — White
Admitted to League: 1921	**Telephone No.:** (0978) 262129
Former Name(s): None	**Ticket Information:** (0978) 262129
Nickname: 'Robins'	**Pitch Size:** 111 x 71yds
Ground: Racecourse Ground, Mold Road,	**Ground Capacity:** 17,500
Wrexham	**Seating Capacity:** 5,026

GENERAL INFORMATION
Supporters Club Administrator: Miss Ena Williams
Address: c/o Club
Telephone Number: (0978) 263111 (Matchdays)
Car Parking: Town Car Parks Nearby
Coach Parking: Crosville Bus Depot
Nearest Railway Station: Wrexham General (Adjacent)
Nearest Bus Station: Wrexham
Club Shop: Centre Spot
Opening Times: Matchdays
Telephone No.: (0978) 263111
Postal Sales: Yes
Nearest Police Station: Bodhyfryd (HQ) (1 mile)
Police Force: Wrexham Division
Police Telephone Number: (0978) 290222

GROUND INFORMATION
Away Supporters' Entrances: Mold End Turnstiles
Away Supporters' Sections: Border Stand, Mold End (covered)
Family Facilities: Location of Stand: None
Capacity of Stand: —
Away Families: None

DISABLED SUPPORTERS INFORMATION
Wheelchairs: Accommodated in Disabled Section on Mold Road side
Disabled Toilets: None
The Blind: Commentaries available

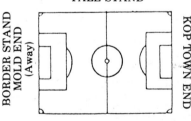

Travelling Supporters Information:
Routes: From North & West: Take A483 and Wrexham Bypass to junction with A541. Branch left and at roundabout follow Wrexham signs into Mold Road; From South & East: Take A525 or A534 into Wrexham then follow A541 signs into Mold Road.

YORK CITY FC

Founded: 1922	**Record Attendance:** 28,123 (5/3/38)
Turned Professional: 1922	**Colours:** Shirts — Red
Limited Company: 1922	Shorts — Blue
Admitted to League: 1929	**Telephone No.:** (0904) 624447
Former Name(s): None	**Ticket Information:** (0904) 624447
Nickname: 'Minstermen'	**Pitch Size:** 115 x 75yds
Ground: Bootham Crescent, York	**Ground Capacity:** 12,760
YO3 7AQ	**Seating Capacity:** 3,059

GENERAL INFORMATION
Supporters Club Administrator: Raymond Wynn
Address: 155 Manor Drive North, York
Telephone Number: (0904) 797578
Car Parking: Street Parking
Coach Parking: By Police Direction
Nearest Railway Station: York (1 mile)
Nearest Bus Station: York
Club Shop:
Opening Times: Monday-Wednesday 9.00-5.00, Thursday-Friday 9.00-1.00, Saturday Matchdays 1.00-3.00 + 4.40-5.30
Telephone No.: (0904) 645941
Postal Sales: Yes
Nearest Police Station: Fulford
Police Force: North Yorkshire
Police Telephone Number: (0904) 631321

GROUND INFORMATION
Away Supporters' Entrances: Grosvenor Road turnstiles
Away Supporters' Sections: Grosvenor Road End, Bootham Crescent
Family Facilities: Location of Stand: None
Capacity of Stand: —

DISABLED SUPPORTERS INFORMATION
Wheelchairs: Accommodated in Disabled Section — in front of Enclosure
Disabled Toilets: Yes
The Blind: Commentaries in Disabled Section

POPULAR STAND

BOOTHAM CRESCENT
GROSVENOR ROAD END
(Away)

SHIPTON STREET

MAIN STAND

Travelling Supporters Information:
Routes: From North: Take A1 then A59 following York signs. Cross Railway Bridge and turn left (2 miles) into Water End. Turn right at end following City Centre signs for nearly ½ mile then turn left into Bootham Crescent; From South: Take A64 and turn left after Buckles Inn on to Outer Ring Road. Turn right on to A19 following City Centre signs for 1½ miles then turn left into Bootham Crescent; From East: Take Outer Ring Road turning left on to A19 then as South; From West: Take Outer Ring Road turning right on to A19, then as South.

ALTRINCHAM FC

Founded: 1903
Limited Company: 1921
Nickname: 'The Robins'
Ground: Moss Lane, Altrincham,
Greater Manchester WA15 8AP

Record Attendance: 10,275 (Feb. 25)
Colours: Shirts — Red and Black Stripes
Shorts — Black
Telephone No.: (061) 928 1045
Pitch Size: 115 x 70yds
Ground Capacity: 6,000
Seating Capacity: 1,000

GENERAL INFORMATION
Supporters Club Administrator: None
Address:
Telephone Number:
Car Parking: Adjacent
Coach Parking: By Police Direction
Nearest Railway Station: Altrincham
(5 mins walk)
Nearest Bus Station: Altrincham
Club Shop:
Opening Times: Matchdays only
Telephone No.: (061) 928 1045
Postal Sales: Yes
Nearest Police Station: Dunham Road,
Altrincham
Police Force: Greater Manchester
Police Telephone Number: (061) 855
4529

GROUND INFORMATION
Away Supporters' Entrances:
Away Supporters' Sections: Chequers End of
Ground
Family Facilities: Location of Stand:
Capacity of Stand:
Away Families:

DISABLED SUPPORTERS INFORMATION
Wheelchairs: Accommodated
Disabled Toilets: None
The Blind: No special facilities

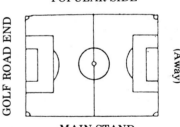

POPULAR SIDE

GOLF ROAD END

CHEQUERS END
(Away)

MAIN STAND
MOSS LANE

Travelling Supporters Information:
Routes: Exit M56 junction 7 following signs Hale and Altrincham. Through 1st set of traffic
lights and take 3rd right — Westminster Road and continue into Moss Lane. Ground on right.

BARROW FC

Founded: 1901
Turned Professional: 1908
Former Name(s): None
Nickname: 'Bluebirds'
Ground: Holker Street, Barrow-in-Furness Cumbria
Record Attendance: 16,840 (1954)

Colours: Shirts — White
         Shorts — Blue
Telephone No.: (0229) 820346
Ticket Information: (0229) 823839
Pitch Size: 110 x 75yds
Ground Capacity: 6,200
Seating Capacity: 1,250

GENERAL INFORMATION
Supporters Club Administrator: E. Smith
Address: 136 Sutherland St., Barrow
Telephone Number: (0229) 837332
Car Parking: Street Parking
Coach Parking: Adjacent to Ground
Nearest Railway Station: Barrow Central (¼ mile)
Nearest Bus Station: ½ mile
Club Shop:
Opening Times: Matchdays only
Telephone No.: (0229) 823061
Postal Sales: Yes
Nearest Police Station: Barrow
Police Force: Cumbria
Police Telephone Number: (0229) 824532

GROUND INFORMATION
Away Supporters' Entrances:
Away Supporters' Sections: None specified
Family Facilities: Location of Stand:

Capacity of Stand: 200
Away Families: Yes

DISABLED SUPPORTERS INFORMATION
Wheelchairs: Accommodated
Disabled Toilets: None
The Blind: None

```
          MAIN STAND
        ┌─────────────┐
 SMALL  │             │ HOLKER
 OPEN   │             │ STREET
 END    │             │
        └─────────────┘
         POPULAR END
```

Travelling Supporters Information:
Routes: Exit M6 junction 36 and take A591 and A590 into Barrow-in-Furness. Turn right at Railway Station — Ground is about ½ mile further along.

BATH CITY FC

Founded: 1889
Former Name(s): None
Nickname: 'City'
Ground: Twerton Park, Bath BA2 1DB
Record Attendance: 18,020 (1960)

Colours: Shirts — Black & White Stripes
Shorts — Black
Telephone No.: (0225) 423087
Ticket Information: (0225) 423087
Pitch Size: 112 x 80yds
Ground Capacity: 9,899
Seating Capacity: 900

GENERAL INFORMATION
Supporters Club: F.O.B. Lounge
Address: c/o Club
Telephone Number: (0225) 313247
Car Parking: Very little space at Ground
Coach Parking: Avon Street, Bath
Nearest Railway Station: Bath Spa (1½ miles)
Nearest Bus Station: Avon Street, Bath
Club Shop:
Opening Times: Matchdays
Telephone No.: (0225) 423087
Postal Sales: Yes
Nearest Police Station: Bath (1½ miles)
Police Force: Avon & Somerset
Police Telephone Number: (0225) 444343

GROUND INFORMATION
Away Supporters' Entrances: Bristol End
Away Supporters' Sections: Bristol End
Family Facilities: Location of Stand:
Family Enclosure
Capacity of Stand: 652

DISABLED SUPPORTERS INFORMATION
Wheelchairs: Accommodated by arrangement — Main Stand
Disabled Toilets: None
The Blind: Commentaries by arrangement

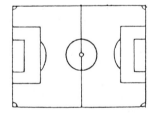

HOME ENCLOSURE
(Covered)

FAMILY ENCLOSURE

BRISTOL END
(Away)

MEMBERS ENCLOSURE
MAIN STAND

Travelling Supporters Information:
Routes: Take the A36 into Bath City Centre. Follow along Pulteney Road then right into Claverton Street and along Lower Bristol Road (A36). Left under railway (1½ miles) into Twerton High Street and ground on left.

BOSTON UNITED FC

Founded: 1934
Former Name(s): Boston Town/Boston Swifts
Nickname: 'The Pilgrims'
Ground: York Street, Boston, Lincs
Record Attendance: 10,086 v Corby Town

Colours: Shirts — Amber with Black Trim
  Shorts — Black
Telephone No.: (0205) 364406
Ticket Information: (0205) 364406
Pitch Size:
Ground Capacity: 14,000
Seating Capacity: 1,769

GENERAL INFORMATION
Supporters Club Administrator: None
Address:
Telephone Number:
Car Parking: At Ground
Coach Parking: At Ground
Nearest Railway Station: Boston (½ mile)
Nearest Bus Station: Boston Coach Station (¼ mile)
Club Shop: 14/16 Spain Place, Boston, Lincs
Opening Times: Weekdays 9.00-4.30
Telephone No.: 0205 364406
Postal Sales: Yes
Nearest Police Station: Boston
Police Force: Lincolnshire
Police Telephone Number: (0205) 366222

GROUND INFORMATION
Away Supporters' Entrances: Town End
Away Supporters' Sections: Town End Enclosure
Family Facilities: Location of Stand: None
Capacity of Stand:
Away Families:

DISABLED SUPPORTERS INFORMATION
Wheelchairs: Accommodated — York Street Stand
Disabled Toilets: None
The Blind: No Special Facilities

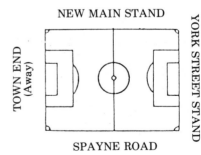

NEW MAIN STAND

TOWN END (Away)

YORK STREET STAND

SPAYNE ROAD

Travelling Supporters Information:
Routes: From North: Take A17 from Sleaford, bear right after railway crossing to traffic lights over bridge. Forward through traffic lights into York Street. From South & West: Take A16 from Spalding and turn right at traffic lights over bridge — forward through traffic lights into York Street.

CHELTENHAM TOWN FC

Founded: 1892
Former Name(s): None
Nickname: 'Robins'
Ground: Whaddon Road, Cheltenham, Glos.
Record Attendance: 8,326 (1956)

Colours: Shirts — Red with White Sleeves
  Shorts — Black with Red & White Trim
Telephone No.: (0242) 521974
Ticket Information: (0242) 573558
Pitch Size: 110 x 73yds
Ground Capacity: 6,000
Seating Capacity: 1,200

GENERAL INFORMATION
Supporters Club Administrator: Paul Wade
Address: c/o Cheltenham Town Social Club
Telephone Number: (0242) 521974
Car Parking: At Ground (120 spaces)
Coach Parking: Wymans Road
Nearest Railway Station: Cheltenham Spa (2 miles)
Nearest Bus Station: Cheltenham, Royal Well
Club Shop: Yes
Opening Times: Matchdays only & office during week
Telephone No.: 0242 521974
Postal Sales: Yes
Nearest Police Station: Whaddon, Cheltenham
Police Force: Gloucestershire
Police Telephone Number: (0242) 528282

GROUND INFORMATION
Away Supporters' Entrances:
Away Supporters' Sections: None specified
Family Facilities: Location of Stand: Gulf Enclosure
Capacity of Stand: 400
Away Families: Yes

DISABLED SUPPORTERS INFORMATION
Wheelchairs: Accommodated
Disabled Toilets: None
The Blind: No Special Facilities

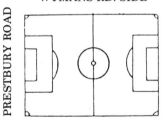

WYMANS RD. SIDE

PRESTBURY ROAD

WHADDON RD. END

MAIN STAND & CAR PARK

Travelling Supporters Information:
Routes: The Ground is situated to the North East of Cheltenham 1 mile from the town centre off the A46 (Prestbury Road) — Whaddon Road is to the East of the A46 just North of Pittville Circus.

COLCHESTER UNITED FC

Founded: 1937
Nickname: 'U's'
Ground: Layer Road Ground, Colchester CO2 7JJ
Record Attendance: 19,072 (27.11.48)

Colours: Shirts — Royal Blue/White Stripes Shorts — White
Telephone No.: (0206) 574042
Pitch Size: 110 x 70yds
Ground Capacity: 6,500
Seating Capacity: 1,169

GENERAL INFORMATION
Supporters Club Administrator: Shaun Whitfield
Address: c/o Club
Telephone Number: (0206) 574042
Car Parking: Street Parking
Coach Parking: Cavalry Barracks (¼ mile)
Nearest Railway Station: Colchester North (2 miles)
Nearest Bus Station: Colchester Town Centre
Club Shop:
Opening Times: Matchdays only
Telephone No.: 0206 578978
Postal Sales: Yes
Nearest Police Station: Queen Street, Colchester (1 mile)
Police Force: Essex
Police Telephone Number: (0206) 762212

GROUND INFORMATION
Away Supporters' Entrances: Layer Road End Turnstiles
Away Supporters' Sections: Layer Road End (covered)
Family Facilities: Location of Stand: Sporting 'U's' — Popular Side
Capacity of Stand: 1,166
Away Families: Yes

DISABLED SUPPORTERS INFORMATION
Wheelchairs: Accommodated by prior arrangement — in front of Main Stand
Disabled Toilets: None
The Blind: Commentaries available

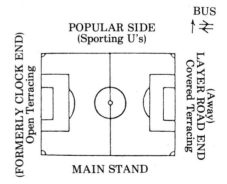

BUS

POPULAR SIDE
(Sporting U's)

(FORMERLY CLOCK END)
Open Terracing

(Away)
LAYER ROAD END
Covered Terracing

MAIN STAND

Travelling Supporters Information:
Routes: From The North: Take A134/B1508 or A12 into Town Centre then follow signs to Layer (B1026) into Layer Road; From South: Take A12 and follow signs to Layer (B1026) into Layer Road; From West: Take A604 or A120 into Town Centre then follow Layer (B1026) signs into Layer Road.

FARNBOROUGH TOWN FC

Founded: 1967
Former Name(s): None
Nickname: 'The Boro'
Ground: John Roberts Ground, Cherrywood Road, Farnborough
Record Attendance: 3,000 (1977)

Colours: Shirts — Yellow with Blue trim
Shorts — Yellow with Blue trim
Telephone No.: (0252) 541469
Ticket Information: (0252) 541469
Pitch Size: 115 x 77yds
Ground Capacity: 4,900
Seating Capacity: 500

GENERAL INFORMATION
Supporters Club Administrator: Vince Curtis
Address: 129 West Heath Road, Farnborough, Hants
Telephone Number: (0252) 548699
Car Parking: Car Park at Ground
Coach Parking: At Ground
Nearest Railway Station: Farnborough (Main), Farnborough North & Frimley
Nearest Bus Station: —
Club Shop: Yes
Opening Times: Matchdays only
Telephone No.: —
Postal Sales: Via Club
Nearest Police Station: Farnborough
Police Force: Hampshire
Police Telephone Number: (0252) 24545

GROUND INFORMATION
Away Supporters' Entrances: Moor Road
Away Supporters' Sections: Moor Road End
Family Facilities: Location of Stand:
None specifically
Capacity of Stand:
Away Families: Yes

DISABLED SUPPORTERS INFORMATION
Wheelchairs: Accommodated
Disabled Toilets: No
The Blind: No Special Facilities

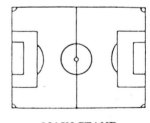

COVERED TERRACES

MOOR ROAD END

PROSPECT ROAD END

MAIN STAND

Travelling Supporters Information:
Routes: Exit M3 junction 4 heading for Frimley and Farnborough. Take 3rd exit at roundabout A325 Farnborough Road. After R.A.E. Sports ground turn right into Prospect Avenue then 2nd right into Cherrywood Road. Ground on right.

GATESHEAD FC

Founded: 1930 (reformed 1977)
Former Name(s): Gateshead Utd.
Nickname: 'Tynesiders'
Ground: International Stadium, Neilson Road, Gateshead NE10 OEF
Record Attendance: 5,012 (20.8.84)

Colours: Shirts — White
Shorts — Black
Telephone No.: (091) 478 3883
Ticket Information: (091) 478 3883
Pitch Size: 106 x 70yds
Ground Capacity: 11,500
Seating Capacity: 11,500

GENERAL INFORMATION
Supporters Club Administrator: Alan Ord
Address: 29 Carryside Close, Whickham, Tyne & Wear
Telephone Number: (091) 488 2873
Car Parking: At Stadium
Coach Parking: At Stadium
Nearest Railway Station: Gateshead Metro (½ mile)
Nearest Bus Station: Gallowgate, Newcastle (2 miles)
Club Shop: Yes — At Stadium
Opening Times:
Telephone No.: (091) 478 5618
Postal Sales:
Nearest Police Station: Gateshead
Police Force: Northumbria
Police Telephone Number: (091) 232 3451

GROUND INFORMATION
Away Supporters' Entrances: None Specified
Away Supporters' Sections: None specified
Family Facilities: Location of Stand: None Specified
Capacity of Stand: 3,300
Away Families: Yes

DISABLED SUPPORTERS INFORMATION
Wheelchairs: Wheelchair lift available in Grandstand
Disabled Toilets: None
The Blind: No Special Facilities

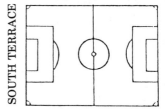

Travelling Supporters Information:
Routes: Take A1(M) to end of Motorway, then exit onto A6115 towards Gateshead. Carry on for 3 miles then carry straight on at roundabout into Park Road. Ground is on right.

KETTERING TOWN FC

Founded: 1875
Former Name(s): None
Nickname: 'The Poppies'
Ground: Rockingham Road, Kettering, Northants
Record Attendance: 11,526 (1947-8)

Colours: Shirts — Red
Shorts — Red
Telephone No.: (0536) 83028/410815
Ticket Information: (0536) 83028
Pitch Size: 110 x 70yds
Ground Capacity: 6,500
Seating Capacity: 2,200

GENERAL INFORMATION
Supporters Club Administrator: None
Address:
Telephone Number:
Car Parking: At Ground
Coach Parking: Cattle Market, Northfield Avenue, Kettering
Nearest Railway Station: Kettering
Nearest Bus Station:
Club Shop: Yes
Opening Times: Matchdays only
Telephone No.: (0536) 83028
Postal Sales:
Nearest Police Station: London Road, Kettering
Police Force: Northants
Police Telephone Number: (0536) 411411

GROUND INFORMATION
Away Supporters' Entrances: None Specified
Away Supporters' Sections: Rockingham Road End
Family Facilities: Location of Stand: None Specified
Capacity of Stand:
Away Families:

DISABLED SUPPORTERS INFORMATION
Wheelchairs: Accommodated — in Main Stand
Disabled Toilets: None
The Blind: No Special Facilities

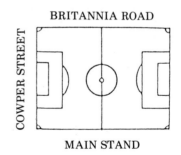

Travelling Supporters Information:
Routes: The Ground is situated to the North of Kettering (1 mile) on the main A6003 Rockingham Road (to Oakham)

KIDDERMINSTER HARRIERS FC

Founded: 1886
Former Name(s): None
Nickname: 'Harriers'
Ground: Aggborough, Hoo Road, Kidderminster, Worcs
Record Attendance: 9,155 (1948)

Colours: Shirts — Red & White Halves
Shorts — White
Telephone No.: (0562) 823931
Ticket Information:
Pitch Size: 112 x 72yds
Ground Capacity: 8,000
Seating Capacity: 400

GENERAL INFORMATION
Supporters Club Administrator:
Address: None
Telephone Number:
Car Parking: At Ground
Coach Parking: At Ground
Nearest Railway Station: Kidderminster
Nearest Bus Station: Kidderminster Town Centre
Club Shop: Yes
Opening Times: Weekdays 9.00-5.00 and match days
Telephone No.: (0562) 823931
Postal Sales: Yes
Nearest Police Station: Habberley Road, Kidderminster
Police Force: West Mercia
Police Telephone Number: (0562) 820888

GROUND INFORMATION
Away Supporters' Entrances:
Away Supporters' Sections: Hoobrook End
Family Facilities: Location of Stand: None specified
Capacity of Stand:
Away Families:

DISABLED SUPPORTERS INFORMATION
Wheelchairs: Accommodated in front of Main Stand
Disabled Toilets: None
The Blind: No Special Facilities

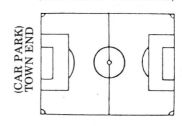

RAILWAY STAND
(BILL GREAVES STAND)

(CAR PARK) TOWN END

(CAR PARK) HOOBROOK ROAD (Away)

MAIN STAND
(HOO ROAD)

Travelling Supporters Information:
Routes: From North & Midlands: Exit M5 (Junction 4) on to A491 then left to A456 and follow Kidderminster signs. When in town turn left at first traffic lights and right at second traffic lights into Hoo Road. From South & West: Exit M5 (Junction 6) and follow signs to Kidderminster (12 miles) (A449) turn right at 1st roundabout then 1st left into Hoo Road.

MACCLESFIELD TOWN FC

Founded: 1875
Former Name(s): Macclesfield FC
Nickname: 'The Silkmen'
Ground: Moss Rose Ground, London Road, Macclesfield, Cheshire
Record Attendance: 10,041 (1948)

Colours: Shirts — Blue
Shorts — White
Telephone No.: (0625) 424324
Ticket Information:
Pitch Size: 110 x 72yds
Ground Capacity: 10,000
Seating Capacity: 600

GENERAL INFORMATION
Supporters Club Administrator: Carole Wood
Address: Warwick Road, Macclesfield
Telephone Number: (0625) 617670
Car Parking: Ample near ground
Coach Parking: Near ground
Nearest Railway Station: Macclesfield (1 ml)
Nearest Bus Station: Macclesfield
Club Shop:
Opening Times: Midweek 7.00-7.30, matchdays 2.00-3.00
Telephone No.: (0625) 613534
Postal Sales: Yes
Nearest Police Station: Macclesfield
Police Force: Cheshire
Police Telephone Number: (0625) 610000

GROUND INFORMATION
Away Supporters' Entrances: Moss Lane
Away Supporters' Sections: Star Lane
Family Facilities: Location of Stand: Family Paddock
Capacity of Stand: 200
Away Families: Yes

DISABLED SUPPORTERS INFORMATION
Wheelchairs: Accommodated in front of stand
Disabled Toilets: None
The Blind: No special facilities

FAMILY ENCLOSURE

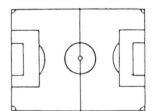

STAR LANE

Travelling Supporters Information:
Routes: Exit M6 Junction 18. Eastwards on A54, then A535 to Chelford. Turn right on to A537 to Macclesfield. Turn right from Chester Road into Crompton Road, then go left at the end along Park Lane (A536), and Park Street. Turn right into Mill Lane (A523 for Leek), then take Cross Street and London Road. Ground on left.

MERTHYR TYDFIL FC

Founded: 1945
Former Name(s): Merthyr Town FC
Nickname: 'Martyrs'
Ground: Penydarren Park, Merthyr Tydfil, Mid Glamorgan
Record Attendance: 21,000 (1949)

Colours: Shirts — White
Shorts — Black
Telephone No.: (0685) 71395
Ticket Information: 0685 4102 - Matchdays
Pitch Size: 110 x 72yds
Ground Capacity: 10,000
Seating Capacity: 1,500

GENERAL INFORMATION
Supporters Club Administrator:
Address: No information
Telephone Number:
Car Parking: Street Parking
Coach Parking: Georgetown
Nearest Railway Station: Merthyr Tydfil (½ mile)
Nearest Bus Station: Merthyr Tydfil
Club Shop:
Opening Times: Matchdays
Telephone No.: (0685) 75125
Postal Sales: Yes
Nearest Police Station: Merthyr Tydfil (¾ ml)
Police Force:
Police Telephone Number:

GROUND INFORMATION
Away Supporters' Entrances: Theatre End
Away Supporters' Sections: Theatre End
Family Facilities: Location of Stand: Family Stand
Capacity of Stand:
Away Families:

DISABLED SUPPORTERS INFORMATION
Wheelchairs: Admitted by prior arrangement
Disabled Toilets: None
The Blind: No Special Facilities

COVERED TERRACING

FAMILY STAND

(PANT-MORLAIS ROAD)
THEATRE END (Away)

MAIN STAND

Travelling Supporters Information:
Routes: From East: Take A465 (High Street) into Pen-y-Darren Road (about 1 ml), ground on right. From West: Take Swansea Road (A4102) past Georgetown and right into Bethesda St., through Pant Morlais Road West into Pen-y-Darren Road. Ground on left.

NORTHWICH VICTORIA FC

Founded: 1874
Former Name(s): None
Nickname: 'The Vics'
Ground: The Drill Field, Drill Field Road, Northwich, Cheshire
Record Attendance: 11,290 (1949)

Colours: Shirts — Green
Shorts — White
Telephone No.: (0606) 41450
Ticket Information: (0606) 41450
Pitch Size: 110 x 73yds
Ground Capacity: 10,000
Seating Capacity: 660

GENERAL INFORMATION
Supporters Club Administrator: James Wood
Address: c/o Club
Telephone Number: (0606) 75964
Car Parking: Street Parking
Coach Parking: Old Fire Station — adjacent
Nearest Railway Station: Northwich
Nearest Bus Station: 100 yds
Club Shop:
Opening Times: Matchdays only
Telephone No.: 0606 41450
Postal Sales: Yes
Nearest Police Station: Chester Way, Northwich
Police Force: Cheshire
Police Telephone Number: (0606) 48000

GROUND INFORMATION
Away Supporters' Entrances: Terminus End
Away Supporters' Sections: Terminus End
Family Facilities: Location of Stand: None Specified
Capacity of Stand:
Away Families:

DISABLED SUPPORTERS INFORMATION
Wheelchairs: Accommodated in front of Main Stand
Disabled Toilets: None
The Blind: No Special Facilities

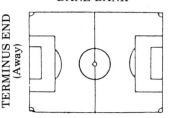

DANE BANK

TERMINUS END (Away)

WATER ST. END

STAND

Travelling Supporters Information:
Routes: From North & South: Exit M6 Junction 19 and take A556. Turn right at second roundabout (A559) and follow road for 1½ miles — ground on right. From East & West: Take A556 to junction with A559 then as North.

REDBRIDGE FOREST FC

Founded: 1979
Former Name(s): Leytonstone-Ilford FC
Nickname: 'The Stones' or 'The Fords'
Ground: Victoria Road, Dagenham, Essex. RM10 7XL
Record Attendance: 7,100 (1967)

Colours: Shirts — Red
Shorts — Red
Telephone No.: (081) 592 1549
Ticket Information: (081) 592 1549
Pitch Size: 112 x 72yds
Ground Capacity: 7,500
Seating Capacity: 450

GENERAL INFORMATION
Supporters Club Administrator:
Address:
Telephone Number:
Car Parking: Car Park at Ground
Coach Parking: Car Park at Ground
Nearest Railway Station: Dagenham East (5 mins walk)
Nearest Bus Station:
Club Shop: No information
Opening Times:
Telephone No.:
Postal Sales:
Nearest Police Station: Dagenham East
Police Force: Metropolitan
Police Telephone Number:

GROUND INFORMATION
Away Supporters' Entrances:
Away Supporters' Sections: Pondfield End
Family Facilities: Location of Stand: Not specified
Capacity of Stand:
Away Families:

DISABLED SUPPORTERS INFORMATION
Wheelchairs: Accommodated ?
Disabled Toilets:
The Blind:

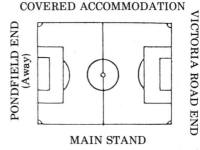

COVERED ACCOMMODATION

PONDFIELD END (Away)

VICTORIA ROAD END

MAIN STAND

Travelling Supporters Information:
Routes: From West: Take A18 or A12 (Eastern Ave) into Dagenham turning right into Whalebone Lane. Branch left at Sports Arena into Wood Lane, then Rainham Road. After ½ mile turn right into Victoria Road for ground. From East: Take A118 or A12 (Eastern Ave) into Dagenham turning left into Whalebone Lane (then as West). From North: Take B174 from Romford straight into Whalebone Lane (then as West from Eastern Ave).

RUNCORN FC

Founded: 1919
Former Name(s): None
Nickname: 'The Linnets'
Ground: Canal Street, Runcorn, Cheshire
Record Attendance: 10,100

Colours: Shirts — Yellow
  Shorts — Green
Telephone No.: (0928) 560076
Ticket Information: (0928) 560076
Pitch Size:
Ground Capacity: 8,400
Seating Capacity: 250

GENERAL INFORMATION
Supporters Club Administrator:
Address: No information
Telephone Number:
Car Parking: At Ground
Coach Parking: At Ground
Nearest Railway Station: Runcorn (1 mile)
Nearest Bus Station:
Club Shop: Yes
Opening Times: Matchdays only
Telephone No.: None
Postal Sales: Yes
Nearest Police Station: Shopping City, Runcorn
Police Force: Cheshire
Police Telephone Number:

GROUND INFORMATION
Away Supporters' Entrances:
Away Supporters' Sections: None Specified
Family Facilities: Location of Stand:
None specified
Capacity of Stand:
Away Families:

DISABLED SUPPORTERS INFORMATION
Wheelchairs: Not Accommodated
Disabled Toilets: None
The Blind: No Special Facilities

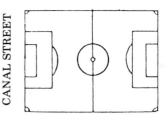

MAIN STAND

CANAL STREET

RIVER END

POPULAR SIDE

Travelling Supporters Information:
Routes: Exit M56 Junction 11 and follow signs, Runcorn, Widnes, Liverpool OR Exit M62 to Widnes and cross over Runcorn & Widnes Bridge taking 2nd exit to ground.

SLOUGH TOWN FC

Founded: 1890
Limited Company: 1991
Former Name(s): Slough, Slough Utd.
Nickname: 'The Rebels'
Ground: Wexham Park Stadium, Wexham Road, Slough SL2 5QR
Record Attendance: 5,000 (1982)

Colours: Shirts — Amber
Shorts — Navy
Telephone No.: (0753) 23358
Ticket Information:
Pitch Size: 117 x 72yds
Ground Capacity: 5,000
Seating Capacity: 395

GENERAL INFORMATION
Supporters Club Administrator: Chris Sliski
Address: 609 Rochford Wharf, Slough, Bucks
Telephone Number: (0753) 531768
Car Parking: Car Park at Ground
Coach Parking: At Ground
Nearest Railway Station: Slough (1 ml)
Nearest Bus Station: Brunel Bus Station (2½ miles)
Club Shop: Yes — In Clubhouse
Opening Times: Matchdays
Telephone No.: 0753 23358
Postal Sales: No
Nearest Police Station: Slough
Police Force: Thames Valley
Police Telephone Number: (0753) 506000

GROUND INFORMATION
Away Supporters' Entrances: North End to right of Clubhouse
Away Supporters' Sections: Training Pitch End/North End
Family Facilities: Location of Stand: None
Capacity of Stand: 395
Away Families:
DISABLED SUPPORTERS INFORMATION
Wheelchairs: Accommodated in front of main stand
Disabled Toilets: In Clubhouse
The Blind: No Special Facilities

CLUBHOUSE
(MAIN STAND)

TRAINING PITCH
NORTH END
(Away)

TOWN END

THE ALLOTMENT SIDE

Travelling Supporters Information:
Routes: From North: M25 Junction 16, East M40 Junction 1, Follow A412 (South) signposted to Slough. A412 through Iver Heath to Crooked Billet (Berni Inn) roundabout, then onto George Green (A412 dual carriageway), Double Century PH on right — George PH on left. Take rightside lane by the footbridge and turn right, Church Lane, ¼ mile turn first left into Norway Drive, follow to end and turn left, Wexham Park Stadium on right. From East: M4 Junction 5, follow A4 London Road, after third set of lights take left side where dual carriageway starts, on right is Co-op Superstore, follow A412 North (Uxbridge Road). This is a roundabout/traffic flow system, this means going to the left then moving right as if going around the roundabout, then left again to take the A412 North. Follow A412 over a rail and canal bridges, after 2nd set lights, ¼ mile take left turn, this is Church Lane. ¼ mile take first then left, Norway Drive follow to end and turn left, Wexham Park Stadium on right. From South: M25 Junction 15 to M4 then Junction 5 and follow directions as from East. From West: M4 Junction 6, turn off left North, roundabout across, Tuns Lane. Turn right at lights, (Fire Station on right), A4 Bath Road, follow East pass Town Hall on right, lights across, roundabout — Brunel Bus Station, keep on, Tesco store on left. Small roundabout, then take left turn, this is Wexham Road.

STAFFORD RANGERS FC

Founded: 1876
Former Name(s): None
Nickname: 'The Boro'
Ground: Marston Road, Stafford
ST16 3BX
Record Attendance: 8,523 (4/1/75)

Colours: Shirts — Black & White Stripes
Shorts — White
Telephone No.: (0785) 42750/54050
Ticket Information: (0785) 42750
Pitch Size: 112 x 75yds
Ground Capacity: 3,472
Seating Capacity: 426

GENERAL INFORMATION
Supporters Club Administrator: Chris Elsley
Address: 326 Sandon Road, Stafford
Telephone Number: (0785) 41954
Car Parking: At Ground
Coach Parking: Chell Road, Stafford
Nearest Railway Station: Stafford (2 miles)
Nearest Bus Station: Stafford
Club Shop: Yes
Opening Times: Matchdays only
Telephone No.: 0785 42750
Postal Sales: Yes
Nearest Police Station: Stafford
Police Force: Staffs
Police Telephone Number: (0785) 58151

GROUND INFORMATION
Away Supporters' Entrances: Lotus End
Away Supporters' Sections: Lotus End
Family Facilities: Location of Stand:
None
Capacity of Stand:
Away Families:

DISABLED SUPPORTERS INFORMATION
Wheelchairs: Accommodated on touchline
Disabled Toilets: None
The Blind: Facilities by arrangement

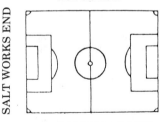

Travelling Supporters Information:
Routes: Exit M6 Junction 14 and take slip road on to A34 straight on at the A34 Island. Take 3rd right into Common Road. 500 yards ahead over bridge — Ground ahead.

TELFORD UNITED FC

Founded: 1877
Former Name(s): Wellington Town FC
Nickname: 'Lillywhites'
Ground: Bucks Head Ground, Watling Street, Wellington, Telford, Shropshire
Record Attendance: 13,000 (1935)

Colours: Shirts — White
Shorts — Blue
Telephone No.: (0952) 223838
Ticket Information: (0952) 223838
Pitch Size: 110 x 75yds
Ground Capacity: 10,000
Seating Capacity: 1,222

GENERAL INFORMATION
Supporters Club Administrator: A. Corbett
Address: c/o Club
Telephone Number: (0952) 255662
Car Parking: At Ground
Coach Parking: At Ground
Nearest Railway Station: Wellington — Telford West
Nearest Bus Station:
Club Shop: Yes
Opening Times: Matchdays only
Telephone No.: 0952 223838
Postal Sales: Yes
Nearest Police Station: Wellington
Police Force: West Mercia
Police Telephone Number: (0952) 290888

GROUND INFORMATION
Away Supporters' Entrances: North Bank Turnstiles
Away Supporters' Sections: North Bank
Family Facilities: Location of Stand: None
Capacity of Stand:
Away Families:

DISABLED SUPPORTERS INFORMATION
Wheelchairs: Accommodated in Terrace areas
Disabled Toilets: None
The Blind: No Special Facilities

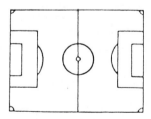

Travelling Supporters Information:
Routes: Exit M54 Junction 6 and take B5061 to Wellington district of town. Ground is on B5061 — formerly the main A5.

WELLING UNITED FC

Founded: 1963
Former Name(s): None
Nickname: 'The Wings'
Ground: Park View Road Ground,
Welling, Kent
Record Attendance: 4,020 (1989/90)

Colours: Shirts — Red with White facings
Shorts — Red
Telephone No.: (081) 301 1196
Ticket Information:
Pitch Size: 112 x 72yds
Ground Capacity: 5,500
Seating Capacity: 500

GENERAL INFORMATION
Supporters Club Administrator: Jim Clench
Address: 1 Westbrooke Crescent, Welling, Kent
Telephone Number: (081) 304 9668
Car Parking: Street Parking only
Coach Parking: Outside Ground
Nearest Railway Station: Welling (¾ mile)
Nearest Bus Station: Bexleyheath
Club Shop: Yes
Opening Times: Matchdays only
Telephone No.: 081 301 1196
Postal Sales: Yes
Nearest Police Station: Welling (¾ mile)
Police Force: Metropolitan
Police Telephone Number: (081) 304 3161

GROUND INFORMATION
Away Supporters' Entrances:
Away Supporters' Sections: Danson Park End
Family Facilities: Location of Stand:
None Specified
Capacity of Stand:
Away Families:

DISABLED SUPPORTERS INFORMATION
Wheelchairs: Accommodated
Disabled Toilets: None
The Blind: No Special Facilities

CRICKET GROUND STAND

PARK VIEW ROAD END

DANSON PARK END (Away)

MAIN STAND

Travelling Supporters Information:
Routes: Take A2 (Rochester Way) from London, then A221 Northwards (Danson Road) to Bexleyheath. At end turn left towards Welling along Park View Road; Ground on left.

WITTON ALBION FC

Founded: 1890
Turned Professional: 1908
Former Name(s):
Nickname: 'Albion'
Ground: Wincham Park, Chapel Street, Wincham, Northwich, CW8 6DA
Record Attendance:

Colours: Shirts — Red and White Stripes
Shorts — Black
Telephone No.: (0606) 43008
Ticket Information:
Pitch Size: 115 x 75yds
Ground Capacity: 5,000
Seating Capacity: 640

GENERAL INFORMATION
Supporters Club Administrator: Caroline Hill
Address: Wincham Park Social Club, Northwich CW8 6DA
Telephone Number: (0606) 47117
Car Parking: 1,200 spaces at Ground
Coach Parking: At Ground
Nearest Railway Station: Northwich
Nearest Bus Station: Northwich
Club Shop:
Opening Times: Matchdays only
Telephone No.: (0606) 43008
Postal Sales: Yes
Nearest Police Station: Northwich
Police Force: Cheshire
Police Telephone Number: (0606) 43541

GROUND INFORMATION
Away Supporters' Entrances: Lostock End
Away Supporters' Sections: Lostock End
Family Facilities: Location of Stand:

Capacity of Stand: 640
Away Families: Yes

DISABLED SUPPORTERS INFORMATION
Wheelchairs: Accommodated
Disabled Toilets: Yes
The Blind: No information

TERRACE STAND

LOSTOCK END
(Away)

WINCHAM END

MAIN STAND

Travelling Supporters Information:
Routes: Exit M6 junction 19 and take A556 towards Northwich. After 3 miles turn right onto A559 following Warrington signs. Turn left opposite Black Greyhound Inn and ground is on left.
Alternative Route: Exit M56 junction 10 and take A559 to Black Greyhound Inn and turn right.

WYCOMBE WANDERERS FC

Founded: 1884
Former Name(s): None
Nickname: 'The Blues' & 'The Chairboys'
Ground: Adams Park, Hillbottom Road, Sands, High Wycombe, Bucks
Record Attendance: 15,678 (1950)

Colours: Shirts — Dark/Light Blue Quarters. Shorts — Navy Blue
Telephone No.: (0494) 472100
Ticket Information: (0494) 472100
Pitch Size: 115 x 75yds
Ground Capacity: 6,000
Seating Capacity: 1,267

GENERAL INFORMATION
Supporters Club Administrator: None
Address:
Telephone Number:
Car Parking: Car Park At Ground (340)
Coach Parking: Car Park At Ground
Nearest Railway Station: High Wycombe
Nearest Bus Station:
Club Shop: Yes
Opening Times: Weekdays & Matchdays
Telephone No.: 0494 472100
Postal Sales: Yes
Nearest Police Station: Queen Victoria Road, High Wycombe (2½ miles)
Police Force: Thames Valley
Police Telephone Number: (0494) 465888

GROUND INFORMATION
Away Supporters' Entrances: Hillbottom Road End
Away Supporters' Sections: Woodland Terrace, Hillbottom Road End
Family Facilities: Location of Stand: 'A' Block — Main Stand
Capacity of Stand: 90
Away Families: Yes

DISABLED SUPPORTERS INFORMATION
Wheelchairs: Accommodated in Main Stand — Pitchside Enclosure
Disabled Toilets: Yes
The Blind: No Special Facilities

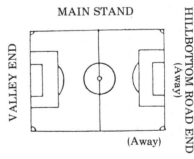

Travelling Supporters Information:
Routes: Exit M40 Junction 4 and take A4010 Road following Aylesbury signs. Go straight on at 3 mini-roundabouts and bear sharp left at 4th roundabout into Lane End Road. Fork right into Hillbottom Road at next roundabout. Ground at end. Hillbottom Road on Sands Industrial Estate. From Town Centre: Take A40 West, after 1½ miles turn left into Chapel Lane (after traffic lights). Turn right then right again at mini-roundabout into Lane End Road — then as above.

YEOVIL TOWN FC

Founded: 1923
Former Name(s): Yeovil & Petters Utd FC
Nickname: 'Glovers'
Ground: Boundary Road, Lufton, Yeovil, Somerset
Record Attendance: 6,153

Colours: Shirts — White & Green Stripes
        Shorts — Green
Telephone No.: (0935) 23662
Ticket Information:
Pitch Size: 115 x 72yds
Ground Capacity: 9,000
Seating Capacity: 4,968

GENERAL INFORMATION
Supporters Club Administrator:
Address: c/o Club
Telephone Number:
Car Parking: Car Parks for 750/1000 Cars
Coach Parking: At Ground
Nearest Railway Station: Yeovil Pen Mill (2½ miles/Yeovil Junction (3½ miles)
Nearest Bus Station: Yeovil (2 miles)
Club Shop: Yes
Opening Times: Monday-Friday 9.30-4.30 and matchdays
Telephone No.: 0935 23662
Postal Sales: Yes
Nearest Police Station: Yeovil
Police Force: Avon
Police Telephone Number: (0935) 75291

GROUND INFORMATION
Away Supporters' Entrances: Copse Road
Away Supporters' Sections: Visitors End
Family Facilities: Location of Stand:
None specified
Capacity of Stand: 4,968
Away Families: Yes

DISABLED SUPPORTERS INFORMATION
Wheelchairs: Accommodated — in Bartlett Stand
Disabled Toilets: Yes
The Blind: No Special Facilities

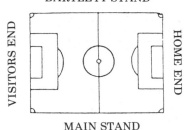

BARTLETT STAND

VISITORS END

HOME END

MAIN STAND

Travelling Supporters Information:
Routes: From London: Take M3 and A303 to Cartgate Roundabout. Enter Yeovil on A3088. Take 1st exit at next roundabout and 1st exit again at next roundabout into Boundary Road. Ground on right after ½ mile. From North: Exit M5 Junction 25 and take A358 (Ilminster) and A303 (Eastbound) entering Yeovil on A3088, then follow directions as London.

DIADORA LEAGUE

AYLESBURY UNITED FC
Founded: 1897. **Nickname:** The Ducks. **Ground:** The Stadium, Buckingham Road, Aylesbury, Bucks. **Ground Capacity:** 7,800. **Seating Capacity:** 400. **Tel. No:** 0296-436350

BASINGSTOKE TOWN FC
Founded: 1896. **Nickname:** "Stoke". **Ground:** Camrose Ground, Western Way, Basingstoke, Hants. **Ground Capacity:** 5,000. **Seating Capacity:** 750. **Tel. No:** 0256 461465 (Office)

BISHOP'S STORTFORD FC
Founded: 1874. **Nickname:** Blues or Bishops. **Ground:** George Wilson Stadium, Rhodes Ave., Bishops Stortford, Herts. **Ground Capacity:** 6,000. **Seating Capacity:** 228. **Tel. No:** 0279 654140

BOGNOR REGIS TOWN FC
Founded: 1883. **Nickname;** The Rocks. **Ground:** Nyewood Lane, Bognor Regis, West Sussex, PO21 2TY. **Ground Capacity:** 6,000. **Seating Capacity:** 230. **Tel. No.** 0243 822325

BROMLEY FC
Founded: 1892. **Ground:** Hayes Lane, Bromley, Kent. **Ground Capacity:** 8,500. **Seating Capacity:** 2,000. **Tel. No:** 0689 34336

CARSHALTON ATHLETIC FC
Founded: 1905. **Nickname:** The Robins. **Ground:** War Memorial Sports Ground, Colston Avenue, Carshalton, Surrey. **Ground Capacity:** 8,000. **Seating Capacity:** 240. **Tel. No:** 081 642 8658/8425

CHESHAM UNITED FC
Founded: 1887. **Former Names:** Chesham Generals & Chesham Town. **Ground:** Amy Lane, Chesham, Bucks. **Ground Capacity:** 5,000. **Seating Capacity:** 150. **Tel. No:** 0494 786661

DAGENHAM FC
Founded: 1949. **Nickname:** The Daggers. **Ground:** Victoria Road, Dagenham, Essex. RM10 7XL. **Ground Capacity:** 7,500. **Seating Capacity:** 640. **Tel. No:** Office 081 592 7194/081 593 3864. Ground: 081 592 1549

ENFIELD FC
Founded: 1893. **Nickname:** 'Ee's'. **Ground:** The Stadium, Southbury Road, Enfield, Middlesex. **Ground Capacity:** 8,500. **Seating Capacity:** 820. **Tel. No:** 081 363 2858

GRAYS ATHLETIC FC
Founded: 1890. **Nickname:** The Blues. **Ground:** Recreation Ground, Bridge Road, Grays, Essex. RM17 6BZ. **Ground Capacity:** 5,500. **Seating Capacity:** 350. **Tel. No:** 0375 391649 (Office) 0375 377753 (Club)

HARROW BOROUGH FC
Founded: 1933. **Former Names:** Roxonians FC, Harrow Town FC. **Nickname:** The Boro. **Ground:** Earlsmead, Carlyon Avenue, South Harrow, Middx. HA2 8SS. **Ground Capacity:** 4,750. **Seating Capacity:** 200. **Tel. No:** 081 422 5221 (Office)

HAYES FC
Founded: 1909. **Former Name** Botwell Mission. **Nickname:** The Missioners. **Ground:** Church Road, Hayes, Middlesex. **Ground Capacity:** 9,500. **Seating Capacity:** 426. **Tel. No:** 081 573 4598

HENDON FC
Founded: 1908. **Nickname:** Dons or Greens. **Ground:** Claremont Road, Cricklewood, London NW2 1AE. **Ground Capacity:** 8,000. **Seating Capacity:** 500. **Tel. No:** 081 455 9185

KINGSTONIAN FC
Founded: 1885. **Former Names:** Kingston & Surbiton YMCA, Saxons, Kingston Wanderers, Kingston-on-Thames, Old Kingstonians. **Nickname:** The K's. **Ground:** Kingsmeadow Stadium, Kingston Road, Kingston Upon Thames, Surrey, KT1 3PB. **Ground Capacity:** 7,000. **Seating Capacity:** 627. **Tel. No:** 081 547 3335

MARLOW FC
Founded: 1870. **Former Name:** Gt. Marlow. **Nickname:** The Blues. **Ground:** Alfred Davis Memorial Ground, Oaktree Road, Marlow, Bucks. **Ground Capacity:** 8,000. **Seating Capacity:** 260. **Tel. No:** 0628 483970

ST. ALBANS CITY FC
Founded: 1908. **Nickname:** The Saints. **Ground:** Clarence Park, Hatfield Road, St. Albans, Herts. **Ground Capacity:** 6,000. **Seating Capacity:** 300. **Tel. No.** 0727 64296

STAINES TOWN FC
Founded: 1892. **Nickname:** Swans. **Ground:** Wheatsheaf Lane, Staines, Middx. **Ground Capacity:** 2,500. **Seating Capacity:** 400. **Tel. No:** 0784 455988

SUTTON UNITED FC
Founded: 1898. **Ground:** Borough Sports Ground, Gander Green Lane, Cheam, Sutton, Greater London. **Ground Capacity:** 8,000. **Seating Capacity:** 1,000. **Tel. No:** 081 644 5120

WINDSOR & ETON FC
Founded: 1892. **Nickname:** The Royalists. **Ground:** Stag Meadow, St. Leonard's Road, Windsor, Berks. SL4 3DR. **Ground Capacity:** 4,500. **Seating Capacity:** 350. **Tel. No:** 0753 860656

WIVENHOE TOWN FC
Founded: 1925. **Nickname:** Dragons. **Ground:** Broad Lane, Elmstead Road, Wivenhoe, Essex. **Ground Capacity:** 3,000. **Seating Capacity:** 200. **Tel. No:** 0206 225380

WOKING FC
Founded: 1889. **Nickname:** Cardinals. **Ground:** Kingsfield Sports Ground, Kingsfield Road, Woking, Berks. **Ground Capacity:** 6,000. **Seating Capacity:** 750. **Tel. No:** 0483 772470

WOKINGHAM TOWN FC
Founded: 1875. **Nickname:** The Town. **Ground:** Finchamstead Road, Wokingham. **Ground Capacity:** 5,000. **Seating Capacity:** 200. **Tel. No:** 0734 780253

HFS LOANS LEAGUE

ACCRINGTON STANLEY FC
Founded: Originally 1876 (Reformed 1968). **Nickname:** 'Stanley' or 'Reds'. **Ground:** Livingstone Road, Accrington, Lancs. **Ground Capacity:** 2,460. **Seating Capacity:** 150. **Tel. No:** 0254 383235

BANGOR CITY FC
Founded: 1876. **Former Name:** Bangor Athletic. **Nickname:** Citizens. **Ground:** Farrar Road, Bangor, Gwynedd. **Ground Capacity:** 10,000. **Seating Capacity:** 900. **Tel. No:** 0248 355852

BISHOP AUCKLAND FC
Founded: 1886. **Nickname:** The Bishops or The Blue's. **Ground:** Kingsway, Bishop Auckland, Co. Durham. **Ground Capacity:** 5,000. **Seating Capacity:** 600. **Tel. No:** 0388 604403

BUXTON FC
Founded: 1877. **Nickname:** The Bucks. **Ground:** The Silverlands, Buxton, Derbys. **Ground Capacity:** 4,000. **Seating Capacity:** 654. **Tel. No:** 0298 24733

CHORLEY FC
Founded: 1883. **Nickname:** 'Magpies'. **Ground:** Victory Park, Duke Street, Chorley, PR7 3DU. **Ground Capacity:** 6,380. **Seating Capacity:** 900. **Tel. No:** 02572 63406

DROYLSDEN FC
Founded: 1892. **Nickname:** The Bloods. **Ground:** Butchers Arms, Market Street, Droylsden, Manchester. **Ground Capacity:** 3,500. **Seating Capacity:** 450. **Tel. No:** 061 370 1426

EMLEY FC
Founded: 1903; **Ground:** Emley Welfare Sports Ground, Emley, Huddersfield, W. Yorks. **Ground Capacity:** 3,000. **Seating Capacity:** 230. **Tel. No:** 0924 848398

FLEETWOOD TOWN FC
Founded: 1977. **Nickname:** The Fishermen. **Ground:** Highbury Stadium, Park Avenue, Fleetwood, Lancs. **Ground Capacity:** 9,500. **Seating Capacity:** 300. **Tel. No:** 0253 876443

FRICKLEY ATHLETIC FC
Founded: 1910. **Former Name:** Frickley Colliery FC. **Nickname:** The Blues. **Ground:** Westfield Lane, South Emsall, Pontefract, W. Yorks. **Ground Capacity:** 6,000. **Seating Capacity:** 800. **Tel. No:** 0977 642460

GAINSBOROUGH TRINITY FC
Founded: 1873. **Nickname:** The Blues. **Ground:** The Northolme, Gainsborough, Lincs. **Ground Capacity:** 9,500. **Seating Capacity:** 350. **Tel. No:** 0427 3295

GOOLE TOWN FC
Founded: 1900. **Nickname:** Town or Vikings. **Ground:** Victoria Pleasure Ground, Carter Street, Goole, North Humbs. **Ground Capacity:** 4,500. **Seating Capacity:** 200. **Tel. No:** 0405 762794 Matchdays only.

HORWICH RMI FC
Founded: 1896. **Nickname:** Railwaymen. **Ground:** Victoria Road, Horwich, Lancs. **Ground Capacity:** 5,000. **Seating Capacity:** 400. **Tel. No:** 0204 696908

HYDE UNITED FC
Founded: 1919. **Nickname:** Tigers. **Ground:** Tameside Stadium, Ewen Fields, Walker Lane, Hyde, Cheshire SK14 2SB. **Ground Capacity:** 4,000. **Seating Capacity:** 400. **Tel. No:** 061 368 1031 (Ground - match days only) 061 368 3687 (Secretary)

LEEK TOWN FC
Founded: 1952. **Nickname:** Blues. **Ground:** Harrison Park, Macclesfield Road, Leek, Staffs. **Ground Capacity:** 3,500. **Seating Capacity:** 400. **Tel. No:** 0538 399278

MARINE FC
Founded: 1894. **Nickname:** Mariners or The Lilywhites **Ground:** Rossett Park, College Road, Crosby, Liverpool 23. **Ground Capacity:** 3,000. **Seating Capacity:** 400. **Tel. No:** 051 924 1743/4046

MATLOCK TOWN FC
Founded: 1885. **Nickname:** The Gladiators. **Ground:** Causeway Lane, Matlock, Derbyshire. **Ground Capacity:** 3,200. **Seating Capacity:** 200. **Tel. No:** 0629 583866 (24hr answering machine) 0629 55362 (match days only)

MORECAMBE FC
Founded: 1920. **Nickname:** Shrimps. **Ground:** Christie Park, Lancaster Road, Morecambe, LA4 4TJ. **Ground Capacity:** 4,500. **Seating Capacity:** 500. **Tel. No:** 0524 411797/417849

MOSSLEY FC
Founded: 1903. **Former Names:** Park Villa 1903-04 Mossley Juniors 1904-09. **Nickname:** The Lilywhites. **Ground:** Seel Park, Market Street, Mossley, Ashton-under-Lyne, Lancs. **Ground Capacity:** 8,000. **Seating Capacity:** 200. **Tel. No:** 0457 832369

SHEPSHED ALBION FC
Founded: 1891. **Former Name:** Shepshed Charterhouse. **Nickname:** The Albion. **Ground:** The Dovecote, Butthole Lane, Shepshed, Leics. **Ground Capacity:** 5,000. **Seating Capacity:** 209. **Tel. No:** 0509 502684

SOUTHPORT FC
Founded: 1881. **Former Names:** Southport Vulcan FC & Southport Central FC. **Nickname:** The Sand Grounders. **Ground:** Haig Avenue, Southport, Lancs. **Ground Capacity:** 6,500. **Seating Capacity:** 1,950. **Tel. No:** 0704 533422

STALYBRIDGE CELTIC FC
Founded: 1911. **Nickname:** Celtic. **Ground:** Bower Fold, Mottram Road, Stalybridge, Cheshire. **Ground Capacity:** 7,500. **Seating Capacity:** 500. **Tel. No:** 061 338 2828

WHITLEY BAY FC
Founded: 1950. **Nickname:** The Bay. **Former Name:** Whitley Bay Athletic. **Ground:** Hillheads Park, Whitley Bay, Northumbria. **Ground Capacity:** 4,500. **Seating Capacity:** 300. **Tel. No:** 091 251 3680 (Ground) 091 251 5179 (Sec.)

BEAZER HOMES PREMIER LEAGUE

ATHERSTONE UNITED FC
Founded: 1979. **Nickname:** The Adders. **Ground:** Sheepy Road, Atherstone, Warwickshire. **Ground Capacity:** 3,500. **Seating Capacity:** 353. **Tel. No:** 0827 717829

BASHLEY FC
Founded: 1947. **Ground:** Recreation Ground, Bashley Common Road, New Milton, Hants. **Ground Capacity:** 4,250. **Seating Capacity:** 200. **Tel. No:** 0425 620280.

BROMSGROVE ROVERS FC
Founded: 1885. **Nickname:** The Rovers. **Ground:** Victoria Ground, 33 Birmingham Road, Bromsgrove, Worcs. **Ground Capacity:** 8,000. **Seating Capacity:** 372. **Tel. No:** 0527 76949

BURTON ALBION FC
Founded: 1950. **Nickname:** The Brewers. **Ground:** Eton Park, Princess Way, Burton-on-Trent, DE14 2RU. **Ground Capacity:** 8,000. **Seating Capacity:** 296. **Tel. No:** 0283 65938

CAMBRIDGE CITY FC
Founded: 1908. **Nickname:** City Devils. **Ground:** City Ground, Milton Road, Cambridge, CB4 1UY. **Ground Capacity:** 5,000. **Seating Capacity:** 400. **Tel. No:** 0223 357973

CHELMSFORD CITY FC
Founded: 1938. **Nickname:** City. **Ground:** The Stadium, New Writtle Street, Chelmsford, Essex. **Ground Capacity:** 2,500 (Due to Safety Certificate). **Seating Capacity:** 500 (Due to Safety Certificate). **Tel. No:** 0245 353052

CORBY TOWN FC
Founded: 1948. **Former Names:** Stewart & Lloyds FC. **Ground:** Rockingham Triangle Stadium, Rockingham Road, Corby, Northants. **Ground Capacity:** 3,000. **Seating Capacity:** 1,150. **Tel. No:** 0536 401007

CRAWLEY TOWN FC
Founded: 1896. **Nickname:** The Reds. **Ground:** Town Mead, Ifield Avenue, West Green, Crawley, Sussex. **Ground Capacity:** 5,000. **Seating Capacity:** 250. **Tel. No:** 0293 21800

DARTFORD FC
Founded: 1888. **Nickname:** The Darts. **Ground:** Watling Street, Dartford, Kent. **Ground Capacity:** 5,750. **Seating Capacity:** 800. **Tel. No:** 0322 73639

DORCHESTER TOWN FC
Founded: 1880. **Nickname:** The Magpies. **Ground:** The Avenue Stadium, Weymouth Ave, Dorchester. DT1 2RY. **Ground Capacity:** 7,210. **Seating Capacity:** 710. **Tel. No:** 0305-262451. **Hotline:** 0839 664412

DOVER ATHLETIC FC
Founded: 1983. **Nickname:** Lillywhites. **Ground:** Crabble Athletic Ground, Lewisham Road, River, Dover, Kent. **Ground Capacity:** 6,500. **Seating Capacity:** 750. **Tel. No:** 0304 822373

FISHER ATHLETIC FC
Founded: 1908. **Nickname:** The 'Fish'. **Ground:** Surrey Docks Stadium, Salter Road, London SE16 1LQ. **Ground Capacity:** 5,700. **Seating Capacity:** 400. **Tel. No:** 071 231 5144 (Office); 071 252 0590 (Club)

GLOUCESTER CITY FC
Founded: 1883. **Former Name:** Gloucester YMCA. **Nickname:** The Tigers. **Ground:** Meadow Park, Sudmeadow Road, Gloucester. **Ground Capacity:** 5,000. **Seating Capacity:** 560. **Tel. No:** 0452 23883

GRAVESEND & NORTH FLEET FC
Founded: 1946. **Nickname:** The Fleet. **Ground:** Stonebridge Road, Northfleet, Gravesend, Kent DA11 9BA. **Ground Capacity:** 6,000. **Seating Capacity:** 400. **Tel. No:** 0474 533796

HALESOWEN TOWN FC
Founded: 1873. **Nickname:** The 'Yeltz'. **Ground:** The Grove, Stourbridge Road, Halesowen, W. Midlands. **Ground Capacity:** 6,000. **Seating Capacity:** 450. **Tel. No:** 021 550 2179

MOOR GREEN FC
Founded: 1901. **Nickname:** The Moors. **Ground:** The Moorlands, Sherwood Road, Hall Green, Birmingham B28 0EX. **Ground Capacity:** 3,000. **Seating Capacity:** 244. **Tel. No:** 021 777 2757

POOLE TOWN FC
Founded: 1880. **Nickname:** The Dolphins. **Ground:** Poole Stadium, Wimborne Road, Poole, Dorset. BH15 2BP. **Ground Capacity:** 6,000. **Seating Capacity:** 1,500. **Tel. No:** 0202 670909

TROWBRIDGE TOWN FC
Founded: 1880. **Nickname:** The Bees. **Ground:** Frome Road Ground, Trowbridge, Wilts. **Ground Capacity:** 5,000. **Seating Capacity:** 200. **Tel. No:** 0225 752076

V.S. RUGBY FC
Founded: 1956. **Former Names:** Valley Sports FC & Valley Sports Rugby FC. **Nickname:** The Valley. **Ground:** Butlin Road, Rugby, Warwickshire, CV21 3ST. **Ground Capacity:** 6,000. **Seating Capacity:** 216 + 24 in Directors Box. **Tel. No:** 0788 543692

WATERLOOVILLE FC
Founded: 1905. **Nickname:** The Ville. **Ground:** Jubilee Park, Aston Road, Waterlooville, Hants. **Ground Capacity:** 6,000. **Seating Capacity:** 560. **Tel. No:** 0705 263867

WEALDSTONE FC
Founded: 1899. **Nickname:** 'Stones' & 'Royals'. **Ground:** Vicarage Road Stadium, Watford, WD1 8ER. **Ground Capacity:** 23,596. **Seating Capacity:** 6,906. **Tel. No:** 081 866 5306 (Office)

WORCESTER CITY FC
Founded: 1908. **Former Names:** Berwick Rangers and Worcester Rovers. **Nickname:** The City. **Ground:** St. Georges Lane, Worcester (WR1 1QT). **Ground Capacity:** 15,000. **Seating Capacity:** 2,500. **Tel. No:** 0905 23003

HAMPDEN STADIUM

Opened: 1903
Location: In the 'Mount Florida' area of Glasgow, South East of the River Clyde
Telephone: Administration (041) 632 1275
Address: Hampden Park, Mount Florida, Glasgow G42 9BA

Ground Capacity: 64,110
Seating Capacity: 11,375
Record Attendance: 150,239 (Scotland v England 17/4/37)
Pitch Size: 115 x 75 yds

GENERAL INFORMATION
Car Parking: Car Park for 1,200 cars at Stadium
Coach Parking: Stadium Car Park
Nearest Railway Stations: Mount Florida & Kings Park (both 5 minutes walk)
Nearest Police Station: Aikenhead Road, Glasgow G42
Police Force Responsible For Crowd Control: Strathclyde
Police Telephone Number: (041) 422 1113

GROUND INFORMATION
Family Facilities: Location of Stand: None
Capacity of Stand:

DISABLED SUPPORTERS INFORMATION
Wheelchairs: Accommodated in Disabled Spectators Terrace: 54 Wheelchairs, 48 Ambulance Seated, 120 Ambulance Standing
Disabled Toilets: Yes, by Disabled Area
The Blind: Personal commentaries from 'Blind Companions'.

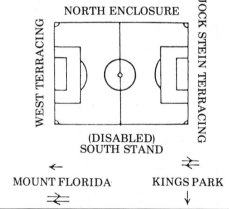

Travelling Supporters Information:
Routes: From the South (Hamilton): Take the A724 to the Cambuslang Road and at Eastfield branch left into Main Street and follow through Burnhill Street and Westmuir Place into Prospecthill Road. Turn left into Aikenhead Road and right into Mount Annan for Kinghorn Drive and the Stadium. From the South (Ayr & Kilmarnock): Take the A77 Fenwick Road, through Kilmarnock Road into Pollokshaws Road then turn right into Langside Avenue. Pass through Battle Place to Battlefield Road and turn left into Cathcart Road. Turn right into Letherby Drive, right into Carmunnock Road and 1st left into Mount Annan Drive for the Stadium. From the North & East: Exit M8 junction 15 and passing Infirmary on left proceed into High Street and cross the Albert Bridge into Crown Street. Join Cathcart Road and proceed South to the end then turn left and left again into Mount Annan Drive for the Stadium.

ABERDEEN FC

Founded: 1903
Former Name(s): None
Nickname: 'The Dons'
Ground: Pittodrie Stadium, Pittodrie Street, Aberdeen

Record Attendance: 45,061 (13/3/54)
Colours: Shirts — Red
Shorts — Red
Telephone No.: (0224) 632328
Ground Capacity: 21,600
Seating Capacity: 21,600

GENERAL INFORMATION
Car Parking: Beach Boulevard, King Street & Golf Road
Coach Parking: Beach Boulevard
Nearest Railway Station: Aberdeen (1 mile)
Nearest Bus Station: Aberdeen
Club Shop: Crombie Sports, Bridge St., Aberdeen
Nearest Police Station: Aberdeen
GROUND INFORMATION
Away Supporters' Sections: Beach End (covered)
DISABLED SUPPORTERS INFORMATION
Wheelchairs: Accommodated in front of Merkland Stand — must be reserved in advance
Disabled Toilets: Between Main Stand and Merkland Stand
The Blind: No Special Facilities

(PITTODRIE STREET)
MAIN STAND
MERKLAND STAND
(GOLF ROAD)
BEACH END (Away)
SOUTH STAND

Travelling Supporters Information:
Routes: From City Centre travel along Union Street then turn left into King Street. Stadium is about ½ mile along King Street (A92) on the right.

AIRDRIEONIANS FC

Founded: 1878
Former Name(s): None
Nickname: 'Diamonds/Waysiders'
Ground: Broomfield Park, Gartlea Road, Airdrie, ML6 9JL

Record Attendance: 24,000 (8/3/52)
Colours: Shirts — Red with White Diamond
Shorts — White
Telephone No.: (0236) 62067
Ground Capacity: 11,830
Seating Capacity: 1,350

GENERAL INFORMATION
Car Parking: Car Park at Ground & Street Parking
Coach Parking: Car Park At Ground
Nearest Railway Station: Airdrie (5 mins walk)
Nearest Bus Station: Airdrie Cross (Adjacent)
Club Shop: No information
Telephone No:
Postal Sales:
Nearest Police Station: Airdrie (500 yards)
GROUND INFORMATION
Away Supporters' Sections: None Specified
DISABLED SUPPORTERS INFORMATION
Wheelchairs: Accommodated — Graham Street Side
Disabled Toilets: None
The Blind: No Special Facilities

GRAHAM STREET
GARTLEA ROAD
WOUTH NIMMO STREET
BROOMFIELD STREET

Travelling Supporters Information:
Routes: From West: Take A89 into Deedes Street and branch right at War Memorial into Alexander Street. Then along Stirling Street into Graham Street and turn right at bus station into Gartlea Road for ground. From East: Take A89 into Forrest Street then take 2nd exit at roundabout across into Clark Street for Graham Street. Turn left at bus station into Garlea Road for ground. From South: Take A73 Carlisle Road to roundabout then 1st exit into Clark Street (then as East). From North: Take A73 Stirling Road to roundabout then 2nd exit across into Motherwell Street. At second roundabout take 3rd exit into Clark Street (then as East).

CELTIC FC

Founded: 1888	**Record Attendance:** 92,000 (1/1/38)
Former Name(s): None	**Colours:** Shirts — Green & White Hoops
Nickname: 'The Bhoys'	Shorts — White
Ground: Celtic Park, 95 Kerrydale Street, Glasgow G40 3RE	**Telephone No.:** (041) 556 2611
	Ground Capacity: 53,033
	Seating Capacity: 8,535

GENERAL INFORMATION
Car Parking: In front of Main Stand and adjacent to Ground
Coach Parking: Adjacent to Ground
Nearest Railway Station: Bridgeton Cross (10 mins walk)
Nearest Bus Station: Glasgow City Centre
Club Shop: Weekdays & Matchdays 9.30-4.30 / Also Celtic Shop, 40 Dundas Street, Glasgow — Monday to Saturday 9.00-5.00
Telephone No: 041 554 4231 (Park) & 041 332 2727 (Dundas Street)
Postal Sales: Yes
Nearest Police Station: Eastern Div. HQ, London Road, Glasgow
GROUND INFORMATION
Away Supporters' Sections: East End
DISABLED SUPPORTERS INFORMATION
Wheelchairs: Accommodated in Enclosure (permit holders only)
Disabled Toilets: North Enclosure
The Blind: Commentaries from 'Blind Partners'

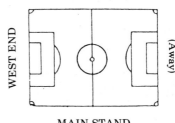

(JANEFIELD STREET)
NORTH ENCLOSURE

WEST END

EAST END
(Away)

MAIN STAND
(LONDON ROAD)

Travelling Supporters Information:
Routes: From South & East: Take A74 London Road towards City Centre, Kerrydale Street is on right about ¼ mile past Belvidere Hospital. From West: Take A74 London Road from City Centre and turn left about ½ mile past Bridgeton Central Station.

DUNDEE UNITED FC

Founded: 1909	**Record Attendance:** 28,000 (Nov. 66)
Former Name(s): Dundee Hibernians	**Colours:** Shirts — Tangerine
Nickname: 'The Terrors'	Shorts — Black
Ground: Tannadice Park, Tannadice Street, Dundee	**Telephone No.:** (0382) 833166
	Ground Capacity: 19,110
	Seating Capacity: 2,252

GENERAL INFORMATION
Car Parking: Street Parking and Gussie Park (100 yards)
Coach Parking: Gussie Park
Nearest Railway Station: Dundee
Nearest Bus Station: Dundee
Club Shop: Forum Centre, Dundee and at ground on matchdays only — Call at office at other times
Nearest Police Station: Bell Street, Dundee
GROUND INFORMATION
Away Supporters' Sections: Arklay Street End
DISABLED SUPPORTERS INFORMATION
Wheelchairs: Accommodated Arklay Street End (Home Supporters Only — on an annual basis)
Disabled Toilets: Tannadice Street Side
The Blind: Annual group pass at Boards Discretion

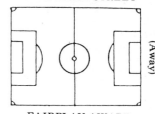

SANDEMAN STREET

ARKLAY ST. END
(Away)

FAIRPLAY AWARD
ENCLOSURE
(TANNADICE STREET)

Travelling Supporters Information:
Routes: Take A972 from Perth (Kingsway West) to Kings Cross Circus Roundabout. Take 3rd exit into Clepington Road and turn right into Provost Road (1 ml) then 2nd left into Sandeman Street for ground.

DUNFERMLINE ATHLETIC FC

Founded: 1885
Former Name(s): None
Nickname: 'The Pars'
Ground: East End Park, Halbeath Road,
Dunfermline, Fife

Record Attendance: 27,816 (30/4/68)
Colours: Shirts — Black and White Stripes
Shorts — Black
Telephone No.: (0383) 724295
Ground Capacity: 19,904
Seating Capacity: 4,011

GENERAL INFORMATION
Car Parking: Street Parking, Car Park at Ground and
Multistorey (10 mins. walk)
Coach Parking: Adjacent to Ground
Nearest Railway Station: Dunfermline (15 mins walk)
Nearest Bus Station: Carnegie Drive, Dunfermline (10
mins walk)
Club Shop: Weekdays 9.30-4.30: Matchdays 1.00-3.00
Nearest Police Station: Holyrood Place, (10 mins walk)
GROUND INFORMATION
Away Supporters' Sections: East Terracing (open) &
North East Enclosure (covered)
DISABLED SUPPORTERS INFORMATION
Wheelchairs: Accommodated in Community Enclosure
Disabled Toilets: None
The Blind: No special facilities

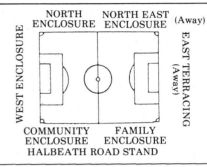

Travelling Supporters Information:
Routes: From Forth Road Bridge and Perth: Exit M90 Junction 3 and take A907 (Halbeath
Road) into Dunfermline — Ground on right. From Kincardine Bridge and Alloa; Take A985 to
A994 then into Dunfermline. Take Pittencrief Street, Glen Bridge and Carnegie Drive to Sinclair
Gardens roundabout. Take 2nd exit into Appin Crescent and continue into Halbeath Road.
Ground on left.

FALKIRK FC

Founded: 1876
Former Name(s): None
Nickname: 'The Bairns'
Ground: Brockville Park, Hope Street,
Falkirk, FK1 5AX

Record Attendance: 23,100 (21/2/53)
Colours: Shirts — Navy Blue
Shorts — White
Telephone No.: (0324) 24121
Ground Capacity: 18,000
Seating Capacity: 2,100

GENERAL INFORMATION
Car Parking: Car Park at Ground (200 cars) & Town
Car Park
Coach Parking: Town Car Park (100 yards)
Nearest Railway Station: Grahamston (100 yards)
Nearest Bus Station: Falkirk Centre (800 yards)
Club Shop: No information
Telephone No:
Postal Sales:
Nearest Police Station: Hope Street, Falkirk (½ mile)
GROUND INFORMATION
Away Supporters' Sections: None Specified
DISABLED SUPPORTERS INFORMATION
Wheelchairs: Accommodated
Disabled Toilets: None
The Blind: No Special Facilities

Travelling Supporters Information:
Routes: From North & West: Exit M876 junction 1 and take A883 into A803 to Falkirk. Pass
along Camelon Road and West Bridge Street and turn left into Hope Street by police station.
Follow along over railway line for ground (about half a mile). From South & East: Take A803
road from Linlithgow into Falkirk along Callendar Road. Pass Callendar Shopping Centre (on
right) along High Street and turn right into Hope Street by police station (then as North &
West)

HEART OF MIDLOTHIAN FC

Founded: 1874
Former Name(s): None
Nickname: 'The Jam Tarts'
Ground: Tynecastle Park, Gorgie Road, Edinburgh EH11 1NL

Record Attendance: 53,496 (13/1/32)
Colours: Shirts — Maroon
Shorts — White
Telephone No.: (031) 337 6132
Ground Capacity: 25,177
Seating Capacity: 10,000

GENERAL INFORMATION
Car Parking: Street Parking in Robertson Ave. and Westfield Road
Coach Parking: Chesser Avenue
Nearest Railway Station: Edinburgh Haymarket (½ mile)
Nearest Bus Station: St. Andrew's Square, Edinburgh
Club Shop: Weekdays 9.30-5.00; Matchdays 10.00-5.00
Telephone No: 031 346 8511
Postal Sales: Yes
Nearest Police Station: Haymarket, Edinburgh
GROUND INFORMATION
Away Supporters' Sections: Gorgie Road Terracing
DISABLED SUPPORTERS INFORMATION
Wheelchairs: Accommodation for 12 Wheelchairs
Disabled Toilets: McLeod Street Side
The Blind: Commentary available

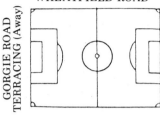

Travelling Supporters Information:
Routes: From West: Take A71 (Ayr Road) into Gorgie Road, ground is about ¾ mile past Saughton Park on left. From North: Take A90 Queensferry Road and turn right into Drum Brae in about ½ mile. Follow Drum Brae into Meadowplace Road (about 1 mile) then Broomhouse Road to junction with Calder Road. Turn right then as from West. From South: Take A702/A703 to A720 (Oxgangs Road). Turn left and follow A720 into Wester Hailes Road (2½ miles) until the junction with Calder Road. Turn right — then as from West.

HIBERNIAN FC

Founded: 1875
Former Name(s): None
Nickname: 'The Hi-Bees'
Ground: Easter Road Stadium, Albion Road, Edinburgh EH7 5QG

Record Attendance: 65,840 (2/1/50)
Colours: Shirts — Green & White
Shorts — White
Telephone No.: (031) 661 2159
Ground Capacity: 27,200
Seating Capacity: 5,896

GENERAL INFORMATION
Car Parking: Adjacent to Ground
Coach Parking: Adjacent to Ground
Nearest Railway Station: Edinburgh Waverley (25 mins walk)
Nearest Bus Station: St. Andrew Square, Edinburgh
Club Shop: None, but goods can be obtained via the ticket office at 178 Easter Road, (Phone 031 652 0630)
Nearest Police Station: Queen Charlotte Street, Leith
GROUND INFORMATION
Away Supporters' Sections: Albion Road Terracing (Open)
DISABLED SUPPORTERS INFORMATION
Wheelchairs: Accommodated in South Enclosure
Disabled Toilets: Albion Road Terracing
The Blind: No special facilities

Travelling Supporters Information:
Routes: From West & North: Take A90 Queensferry Road to A902 and continue for 2¼ miles. Turn right into Great Junction Street and follow into Duke Street then Lochend Road. Turn sharp right into Hawkhill Avenue at Lochend Park and follow road into Albion Place for ground. From South: Take A1 through Musselburgh (Milton Rd/Willow Brae/London Road) and turn right into Easter Road after about 2½ miles. Take 4th right into Albion Road for ground.

Motherwell FC

Founded: 1886
Former Name(s): None
Nickname: 'The Well'
Ground: Fir Park, Fir Park Street
Motherwell ML1 2QN

Record Attendance: 35,632 (12/3/52)
Colours: Shirts — Amber & Claret
Shorts — Claret
Telephone No.: (0698) 61437/8
Ground Capacity: 18,000
Seating Capacity: 3,500

GENERAL INFORMATION
Car Parking: Street Parking and nearby car parks
Coach Parking: By Police Direction
Nearest Railway Station: Motherwell (1½ miles)
Nearest Bus Station: Motherwell
Club Shop: Weekdays 9.30-4.30; Saturdays 10.00-5.30
(Matchdays)
Nearest Police Station: Motherwell (¼ mile)
GROUND INFORMATION
Away Supporters' Sections: Dalzeel Gate End
DISABLED SUPPORTERS INFORMATION
Wheelchairs: Accommodated by prior consent of
Secretary
Disabled Toilets: None
The Blind: No special facilities

KNOWETOP AVENUE

DALZEEL GATE (Away)

MAIN STAND
(FIR PARK STREET)

Travelling Supporters Information:
Routes: From East: Take A723 into Merry Street and turn right into Brondon Street (1 mile).
Follow through to Windmill Hill and turn right at Fire Station into Knowetop Avenue for
ground. From elsewhere: Exit M74 Junction 4 and take A723 Hamilton Road into Town Centre.
Turn right into Brondon Street then as from East.

Rangers FC

Founded: 1873
Former Name(s): None
Nickname: 'The Gers/Light Blues'
Ground: Ibrox Stadium, 150 Edmiston Drive,
Glasgow G51 3XD

Record Attendance: 118,567 (2/1/39)
Colours: Shirts — Blue
Shorts — White
Telephone No.: (041) 427 8500
Ground Capacity: 43,000 (from 12/91)
Seating Capacity: 41,000 (from 12/91)

GENERAL INFORMATION
Car Parking: New facilities to be announced
Coach Parking: Albion training ground
Nearest Railway Station: Ibrox (Underground) 2 mins
walk)
Nearest Bus Station: Glasgow City Centre
Club Shop: The Rangers Shop, Copland Road,
Glasgow, Monday-Saturday 9.00-5.00
Postal Sales: Yes
Nearest Police Station: Orkney Street, Glasgow
GROUND INFORMATION
Away Supporters' Sections: Broomloan Road Stand
DISABLED SUPPORTERS INFORMATION
Wheelchairs: Accommodated in front of West
Enclosure
Disabled Toilets: West End of West Enclosure
The Blind: Commentaries East End of West Enclosure

BROOMLOAN ROAD STAND (Away)

(WEST) GOVAN STAND (EAST)

COPLAND ROAD STAND

WEST MAIN STAND EAST
EDMISTON DRIVE

Travelling Supporters Information:
Routes: From All Parts: Exit M8 at B768 turn-off for Govan. Road leads straight to Stadium.

126

St. Johnstone FC

Founded: 1884	**Record Attendance:** 10,504 (1990/91)
Former Name(s): None	**Colours:** Shirts — Blue
Nickname: 'Saints'	Shorts — White
Ground: McDiarmid Park, Crieff Road,	**Telephone No.:** (0738) 26961
Perth PH1 2SJ	**Ground Capacity:** 10,721
	Seating Capacity: 10,721

GENERAL INFORMATION
Car Parking: Car Park at Ground
Coach Parking: At Ground
Nearest Railway Station: Perth (3 miles)
Nearest Bus Station: Perth (3 miles)
Club Shop: Yes
Nearest Police Station: Perth (1½ miles)
GROUND INFORMATION
Away Supporters' Sections: North Stand and North End of West Stand
DISABLED SUPPORTERS INFORMATION
Wheelchairs: Accommodated in Disabled areas of West and East Stands
Disabled Toilets: In both areas
The Blind: Audio Facilities

WEST STAND
(MAIN STAND)

ORMOND STAND

NORTH STAND
(Away)

EAST STAND

Travelling Supporters Information:
Routes: Take A9 Inverness Road north from Perth. Ground is beside dual-carriageway, — Perth Western By-Pass.

St. Mirren FC

Founded: 1877	**Record Attendance:** 47,428 (7/3/25)
Former Name(s): None	**Colours:** Shirts — Black & White Stripes
Nickname: 'The Saints/The Buddies'	Shorts — White
Ground: St. Mirren Park, Love Street,	**Telephone No.:** (041) 889 2558
Paisley PA3 2EJ	**Ground Capacity:** 25,844
	Seating Capacity: 1,800 (to increase 1991/92)

GENERAL INFORMATION
Car Parking: Street Parking
Coach Parking: Racecourse — Paisley
Nearest Railway Station: Paisley Gilmour Street (400 yards)
Nearest Bus Station: Paisley
Club Shop: Weekdays 9.30-5.00; Saturday 9.30-2.00
Telephone No: 041 887 0902
Postal Sales: Yes
Nearest Police Station: Mill Street, Paisley (1 mile)
GROUND INFORMATION
Away Supporters' Sections: North Bank
DISABLED SUPPORTERS INFORMATION
Wheelchairs: Accommodated in front of Main Stand (West)
Disabled Toilets: Beside Main Stand (East)
The Blind: No special facilities

NORTH BANK (Away)

WEST TERRACING

EAST TERRACING
(LOVE STREET)

MAIN STAND
(ALBION STREET)

Travelling Supporters Information:
Routes: From All Parts: Exit M8 junction 29 and take A760 Paisley Road. Ground approx. ½ mile along.

SCOTTISH FOOTBALL LEAGUE
1st and 2nd DIVISION CLUBS

ALBION ROVERS FC
Founded: 1882. Nickname: Wee Rovers. Ground: Cliftonhill Stadium, Main Street, Coatbridge, ML5 3RB. Correspondence: c/o 21 Academy St., Coatbridge. Record Attendance: 27,381 v Rangers 8.2.36. Ground Capacity: 3,496. Seating Capacity: 538. Tel. No. 0236 32350

ALLOA FC
Founded: 1883. Nickname: The Wasps. Ground: Recreation Park, Clackmannan Rd, Alloa, FK10 1RR. Record Attendance: 13,000 v Dunfermline 26.2.39. Ground Capacity: 3,100. Seating Capacity: 450. Tel. No. 0259 722695

ARBROATH FC
Founded: 1878. Nickname: The Red Lighties. Ground: Gayfield Park, Queens Drive, Arbroath, DD11 1QB. Record Attendance: 13,510 v Rangers 23.2.52. Ground Capacity: 5,773. Seating Capacity: 715. Tel. No. 0241 72157

AYR UNITED FC
Founded: 1910. Former Names: Ayr Parkhouse & Ayr FC (Amalgamated in 1910). Nickname: The Honest Men. Ground: Somerset Park, Tryfield Place, Ayr, KA8 9NB. Record Attendance: 25,225 v Rangers 13.9.69. Ground Capacity: 15,873. Seating Capacity: 1,593. Tel. No: 0292 263435

BERWICK RANGERS FC
Founded: 1881. Nickname: The Borderers. Ground: Shielfield Park, Tweedmouth, Berwick-on-Tweed, TD15 2EF. Record Attendance: 13,365 v Rangers 28.1.67. Ground Capacity: 3,760. Seating Capacity: 1,475. Tel. No: 0289 307424

BRECHIN CITY FC
Founded: 1906. Nickname: The City. Ground: Glebe Park, Trinity Road, Brechin, Angus, DD9 6BJ. RECORD ATTENDANCE: 8,244 v Aberdeen 3.2.73. Ground Capacity: 2,800. Seating Capacity: 290. Tel. No: 03562 2856

CLYDE FC
Founded: 1878. Nickname: Bully Wee. Ground: (for 1991/91) Douglas Park, Douglas Park Lane, Hamilton. ML3 ODF. Record Attendance: (At present ground) 28,690 v Hearts (3/3/37) Ground Capacity: 9,168. Seating Capacity: 1,575. Tel. No: 041 221 7669

CLYDEBANK FC
Founded: 1965. Nickname: The Bankies. Ground: Kilbowie Park, Arran Terrace, Clydebank, G81 2PB. Record Attendance: 14,900 v Hibernian 10.2.65. Ground Capacity: 9,950. Seating Capacity: 9,950. Tel. No: 041 952 2887

COWDENBEATH FC
Founded: 1881. Nickname: Cowden. Ground: Central Park, Cowdenbeath, KY4 9EY. Record Attendance: 25,586 v Rangers 21.9.49. Ground Capacity: 10,000 (Restricted). Seating Capacity: 2,000. Tel. No: 0383 511205

DUMBARTON FC
Founded: 1872. Nickname: Sons. Ground: Boghead Park, Miller Street, Dumbarton, G82 2JA. Record Attendance: 18,000 v Raith Rovers 2.3.57. Ground Capacity: 9,500. Seating Capacity: 750. Tel. No: 0389 62569

DUNDEE FC
Founded: 1893. Nickname: The Dark Blues. Ground: Dens Park Stadium, Dens Road, Dundee DD3 7JY. Record Attendance: 43,024. Ground Capacity: 22,320. Seating Capacity: 11,900. Tel. No: 0382 826104

EAST FIFE FC
Founded: 1903. Nickname: The Fifers. Ground: Bayview Park, Methil, Fife, KY8 3AG. Record Attendance: 22,515 v Raith Rovers 2.1.50. Ground Capacity: 5,150. Seating Capacity: 600. Tel. No: 0333 26323

EAST STIRLINGHSIRE FC
Founded: 1881. Former Name: Bainsford Blue Bonnets. Nickname: The Shire. Ground: Firs Park, Firs Street, Falkirk, FK2 7AY. Record Attendance: 11,500 v Hibernian 10.2.60. Ground Capacity: 4,000. Seating Capacity: 200. Tel. No: 0324 23583

FORFAR ATHLETIC FC
Founded: 1885. Nickname: Sky Blues or Loons. Ground: Station Park, Carseview Road, Forfar. Correspondence: c/o 4 Kayarine Street, Forfar, Tayside DD8 3JZ. Record Attendance: 10,780 v Rangers 2.2.70. Ground Capacity: 8,388. Seating Capacity: 739. Tel. No: 0307 63576

GREENOCK MORTON FC
Founded: 1874. Nickname: Ton. Ground: Cappielow Park, Sinclair St., Greenock, PA15 2TY. Record Attendance: 23,500 v Celtic 29.4.21. (Also v Rangers 21.2.53). Ground Capacity: 14,868. Seating Capacity: 5,518. Tel. No: 0475 23571

HAMILTON ACADEMICALS FC
Founded: 1874. Nickname: The Accies. Ground: Douglas Park, Douglas Park Lane, Hamilton, ML3 ODF. Record Attendance: 28,690 v Hearts 3.3.37. Ground Capacity: 9,168. Seating Capacity: 1,575. Tel. No: 0698 286103

KILMARNOCK FC
Founded: 1869. Nickname: Killie. Ground: Rugby Park, Rugby Road, Kilmarnock, KA1 2DP. Record Attendance: 34,246 v Rangers 17.8.63. Ground Capacity: 17,300. Seating Capacity: 5,050. Tel. No: 0563 25184

MEADOWBANK THISTLE FC
Founded: 1943. Former Name: Ferranti Thistle FC. Nickname: Thistle or 'Wee Jags'. Ground: Meadowbank Stadium, London Road, Edinburgh EH11 1UL. Correspondence: 52 Stewart Terrace, Edinburgh EH11 1UL. Record Attendance: 4,200 v Albion Rovers 9.9.74. Ground Capacity: 15,500. Seating Capacity: 8,000. Tel. No: Office 031 337 2442 Ext.3666. Ground 031 661 5351.

MONTROSE FC
Founded: 1879. Nickname: Gable Endies. Ground: Links Park, Wellington Street, Montrose, DD10 8QD. Correspondence: 50 High Street, Montrose, DD10 8JF. Record Attendance: 8,983 v Dundee 17.3.73. Ground Capacity: 6,500. Seating Capacity: 280. Tel. No: 0674 73200

PARTICK THISTLE FC
Founded: 1876. Nickname: The Jags. Ground: Firhill Park, 90 Firhill Road, Glasgow G20 7AL. Record Attendance: 49,838 v Rangers 18.2.22. Ground Capacity: 16,614. Seating Capacity: 2,900. Tel. No: 041 945 4811

QUEEN OF THE SOUTH FC
Founded: 1919. Nickname: The Doonhamers. Ground: Palmerston Park, Terregles St., Dumfries DG2 9BA. Record Attendance: 24,500 v Hearts 23.2.52. Ground Capacity: 6,750. Seating Capacity: 1,357. Tel. No: 0387 54853

QUEENS PARK FC
Founded: 1867. Nickname: The Spiders. Ground: Hampden Park, Mount Florida, Glasgow G42 9BA. Record Attendance: Club -95,772 v Rangers 18.1.30. Ground - 150,239 Scotland v England 17.4.37. Ground Capacity: 64,110. Seating Capacity: 11,375. Tel. No: 041 632 1275

RAITH ROVERS FC
Founded: 1883. Nickname: The Rovers. Ground: Stark's Park, Pratt Street, Kirkcaldy, KY1 1SA. Record Attendance: 31,306 v Hearts 7.2.53. Ground Capacity: 8,592. Seating Capacity: 3,020. Tel. No: 0592 263514

STENHOUSEMUIR FC
Founded: 1884. Nickname: Warriors. Ground: Ochilview Park, Gladstone Rd., Stenhousemuir, FK5 5QL. Correspondence: A.T. Bulloch, Secretary, 20 Findhorn Place, Hallglen, Falkirk, Stirlingshire FK1 2QJ. Record Attendance: 12,500 v East Fife 11.3.50. Ground Capacity: 4,000. Seating Capacity: 340. Tel. No: 0324 562992

STIRLING ALBION FC
Founded: 1945. Nickname: The Albion (or The Binos). Ground: Annfield Park, 23 St. Ninians Road, Stirling, FK8 2HE. Record Attendance: 28,600 v Celtic 14.3.59. Ground Capacity: 10,000. Seating Capacity: 400. Tel. No: 0786 50399

STRANRAER FC
Founded: 1870. Nickname: The Blues. Ground: Stair Park, London Road, Stranraer, DG9 8BS. Correspondence: c/o 28 Springfield Cl., Stranraer, DG9 7QV. Record Attendance: 6,500 v Rangers 24.1.48. Ground Capacity: 5,000. Seating Capacity: 700. Tel. No: 0776-3271 (Secretary - Home 0776 2194)

WORLD'S GREATEST SOCCER MAGAZINE

WRITTEN BY THOSE IN THE KNOW... FOR THOSE WHO'D LIKE TO BE

LEADING THE WAY FOR 40 YEARS!

OTHER BOOKS FROM:

SOCCER BOOK

PUBLISHING LIMITED

FOOTBALL IN EUROPE 1990/91
(published October 1991)

Contains masses of results, league tables, internationals etc. for the 1990/91 season in Europe.

Softback Price £9.99
(Postage £1.25)

50 YEARS OF FA CUP FINALS
1883-1932

The first book in our 'Classic Reprint Series' was initially published in 1932 and original copies now change hands for over £50. Contains team photos, write-ups, line-ups and scorers for the FA Cup Finals 1883-1932.

Softback Price £6.99
(Postage 95p)

Order direct from:

SOCCER BOOK PUBLISHING LIMITED

(Dept. SG8)

72 St. Peters Avenue, Cleethorpes, DN35 8HU, England